John Dee

of

Mortlake

(1527-1609)

Nicholas Dakin

Nicholas Dakin 18.X.2011

Barnes and Mortlake History Society 2011

ISBN 978-0-9542038-6-3

First published by Barnes and Mortlake History Society
October 2011

Printed and bound by printondemand.com

www.barnes-history.org.uk

Portrait of John Dee

A marvellous neutrality have these things mathematical, and also strange participation between things supernatural, immortal, intellectual, simple and indivisible, and things natural, mortal, sensible, compounded and divisible.

John Dee: *Mathematical Preface* to Henry Billingsley's translation of Euclid's *Elements of Geometry* (1570)

Contents

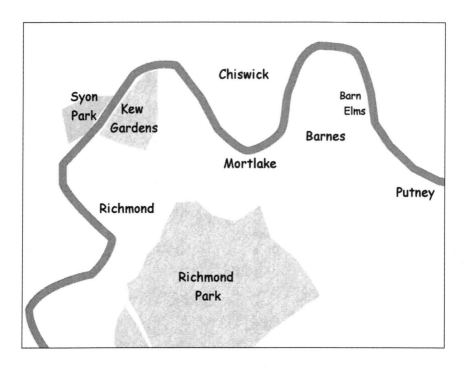

Map showing the location of Mortlake on the banks of the River Thames

Foreword

There is a growing body of work on Dr John Dee, some of it impressively scholarly. This fascinating figure is now firmly identified with mainstream intellectual life in 16th century Europe, and the old accusations of wizardry, sorcery and necromancy have been silenced it seems for ever.

Dee, first and foremost, was a natural philosopher – a scientist in effect – who came to believe that he could arrive at a closer understanding of God's creation through contact with angels. He was also a political advisor and an astronomer, an antiquarian and bibliophile, a classicist and linguist; he designed stage machinery and instructed in mathematics, navigation and engineering, and his reputation in Europe as an astrologer and alchemist was considerable. For all these reasons, it is far more helpful to regard him as a Renaissance polymath than a medieval magus; and if a literary model is required, he is surely Shakespeare's Prospero, not Marlowe's Faustus.

Given the remit of a local historian, it has not been my task, even if I had had the time, ability and erudition, to advance the cause of John Dee with fresh insights and new primary sources. At first the idea was simply to take the 400th anniversary of Dee's death – 2009 by the way, not 2008 – and Dilys Henrik Jones's out-of-print biography of Dee (published by the Barnes and Mortlake History Society in 1995) as points of departure. I also needed to come up with material for a public lecture. But as the process of writing became less and less an editorial task and more and more my own voyage of discovery, I came to the conclusion that I wanted to do more justice to 16th century Mortlake and the remarkable house with its laboratories, library and oratory that had once stood there. I also wanted to create some impression of the Dee household and place its mistress, Jane Dee, momentarily on the same footing as her husband. In other words more colour and detail were necessary.

I hope I have supplied them. I hope, too, that what follows is readable and, to a point, convincing as a history of the early modern period. Yet I am very sensitive to the fact that so much has been compressed or omitted. Nowhere is this more so than when I presume to write – and not write – on Dee as a scientist, mathematician and mystic.

I take full responsibility for that; and so prefer to thank instead Mike Smith, sometime Chairman of the Barnes and Mortlake History Society, who first suggested the project and offered subsequent encouragement; also Jane Edwards, Claire Davies, Murray Hedgcock, Paul Rawkins and David and Helen Deaton.

Claire is owed a particular debt of thanks, both for hosting and chairing various meetings and also for locating important Dee images. She and David Deaton carried out the essential task of preparing the text for publication. David also offered useful initiation into the technical mysteries of electronic book production. Finally, Jane Baxter was most helpful when I paid a number of visits to the Richmond Local Studies Centre.

Then, sadly, linger those shades from the past: Dilys Henrik Jones herself; my old friend Richard Jeffree, who introduced me many years ago to the Barnes and Mortlake History Society; and those two great Mortlake historians, Charles Hailstone and Leslie Freeman.

And lastly, but really firstly, my own 'paineful' wife, Milena, to whom much love and gratitude.

Nicholas Dakin

Sources

I am indebted here to the work of Dilys Henrik Jones, whose biography *John Dee, the Magus of Mortlake*, published in 1995, is now out of print. This is a good opportunity to pay tribute to its clarity, compression and general usefulness.

I have also relied on Benjamin Woolley's excellent *The Queen's Conjuror,* Julian Roberts' admirably succinct contribution to the *Oxford Dictionary of National Biography,* William Sherman's impressive *John Dee, The Politics of Reading and Writing in the English Renaissance,* and Julian Roberts' and Andrew Watson's edition of Dee's 1583 Library Catalogue.

The four primary sources, however, for any biography of Dee are:

1. The *Ephemerides* of Stadius, an astronomical almanac for the years 1554-1600. Dee used his copy (Bod.Mss Ashmole 487) from 1577 for making personal records.

2. The *Ephemerides* of Maginus (Bod.Mss Ashmole 488), another almanac. This contained data for the years 1581-1620. Dee used this from September 1589.

Both almanacs were discovered in the Ashmolean collection at Oxford in the late 1830s. They were subsequently combined, edited and heavily abridged by James Orchard Halliwell in 1842 for the Camden Society. A handy modern version, less heavily abridged, was produced by Edward Fenton in 1998 (*The Diaries of John Dee*, Day Books).

3. The 'Spirit Diaries' (1581 onwards). Dee's own transcripts of what his Scryers saw and heard in the show stone. He took down what they dictated as the 'conversations' were in progress, later writing up a fair copy.

Unabridged, these could take up as much as five volumes. The first edition was that of Meric Casaubon (1659), using only the buried material that was dug up by the bibliophile and antiquary Sir Robert Cotton. In modern times CL *Whitty* has made a full transcript.

4. *The Compendious Rehearsall of John Dee his Dutiful Declaration and Proof of the Course and Race of his Studious Lyfe.*

This is Dee's petition in 1592 to Queen Elizabeth.

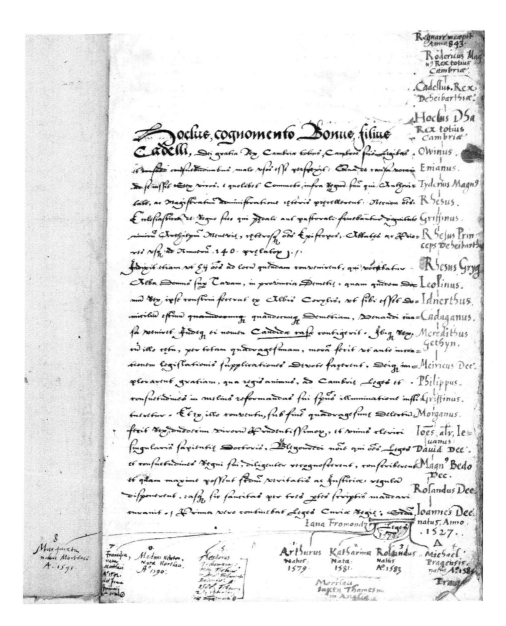

Genealogical notes in Dee's copy of *The Laws of Hywel Dada*

10

Prologue

At 4.15pm on 20 March 1607, at the house of Mistress Goodman somewhere in the City of London, Dr John Dee, now in his eightieth year, began what was to prove his last series of 'angelic conversations'. His final scryer, Bartholomew Hickman, had also been one of his first, long ago in the summer of 1579.[1] But this time only the angel Raphael deigned to appear in the crystal show stone and speak. Hickman dictated while Dee scribbled furiously. Later that night, as was always his custom, Dee wrote them up in the Spirit Diary:

> **Raphael:** *I am blessed Raphael: John Dee, I am sent of God for comfort first to certify thee thou shalt overcome this thy infirmity . . . Ask at your will.*
>
> **Δ:**[2] *Oh God, I am to enter into a great attempt, to make the council privy of my beggary, and to offer to the Earl of Salisbury such my duties as I may perfect to his content.*[3] *How standeth this with your good liking?*
>
> **Raphael:** *Proceed in thy suit so shortly as thou canst find thy health and body able.*
>
> **Δ:** *Of the blood, not coming out at my fundament, but a little, as it were a pinhole of the skin?*
>
> **Raphael:** *For the cure and thy help for the stone, God will work thee in thy heart and mind, and restore thee to health again . . .*

An old man's concern for his piles (severe it would seem) and a troublesome kidney stone are a far cry from the 'angelic actions' of the 1580s and the visions *in crystallo* transmitted by Edward Kelley, the greatest and most notorious of all Dee's scryers. Yet the old complaint of poverty and the lifelong search for preferment and patronage are even here present, and it is sad to think that these last days of John Dee were if anything more straitened. There is even the suspicion that Hickman, like Kelley before him, is playing on the old man's credulity and insecurity.

In later conversations in July, Raphael renewed the old promises of delivering finally the philosopher's stone and initiating Dee into a 'perfect understanding of the hid knowledge and secrecy of God'. He next reminded Dee that although God had allowed him to live to a great age, the 'course of nature for age' – death - was inescapable. But God, who had so prolonged the life of Hezekiah in the Old Testament, would grant Dee a similar extension. There would be time for one final journey.

Dee, the spirit continued, would have to set his affairs in order. His eldest and now only surviving daughter Katherine was to accompany him ('thou canst not be without her'). There would be 'a very honest and well disposed young man' and also one John Pontoys to complete the party.[4] Finally Arthur Dee, the eldest and now the only surviving son, was to be encouraged to undertake a journey of his own overseas. Do we sense here a deliberate attempt to separate the surviving members of the family and send them beyond the protection of English law?

Back in Mortlake, after dinner at about half past four on July 17, Dee went over to the cedar wood chest in which he had long kept his most precious mystical books and apparatus and took out his 'jewel', the crystal stone he had used before the Emperor Rudolf II in Prague some twenty years previously. Set now in gold, it was shown to Hickman. Dutiful as ever, Raphael soon appeared:

Raphael: *In the name of Jesus Christ . . . I have now, here, in this pearl entered possession, in token hereafter to be that blessed creature, to be obedient unto God's commandment, to serve thee at all times, when thou art placed in thy journey, which God hath commanded thee . . .*

More than a month passed. Then on 5 September, at half past nine in the evening, there was renewed contact:

Hickman: *He is in the stone now.*
Raphael: *John Dee, such hath God's mercies been in suffering wicked men to prevail against thee . . . that although they (most wickedly) have robbed thee of thy possessions, yet God would not suffer those wicked ones by any of their malicious practices to prevail in any wise to hurt thy body.*

Once more there is the suspicion that Hickman is playing on an old man's sense of grievance. It happens yet again when Dee frets over the disappearance of his 'silver double gilt bell-salt' and his son Arthur is unjustly incriminated.[5] Raphael also makes light of Dee's leaving the Mortlake house:[6]

Thou shalt be better able in health and strength of thy body to come into England again, if thou wilt: but thou shalt see and perceive thyself so mercifully provided for, that thou wilt have but little mind or willingness to come into England again, such shall God's great mercies be towards thee.
Δ: Then I perceive that I shall not make any great account of keeping my house at Mortlake for my return hither.

This journey, with its promise of success, never took place. Perhaps Dee was too infirm to make it. There is also a grim, even deliberate, irony in Raphael's words. The journey, we now realise, has become metaphorical: it is a journey towards death . . .

The above comes almost entirely from the spirit diaries of John Dee. In so far as they are an account of how one of the most brilliant intellects of the Elizabethan Age came to be duped by fraudsters, they are remarkable documents full of human interest. Together with the jottings that are found everywhere in Dee's almanacs, they constitute one of the first private diaries in the English language. Many of the events, recorded just as they were happening, have even after four hundred years an extraordinary immediacy.

**Dee's Diary for November 1577, notes made in the margins of
Joannes Stadius's *Ephemerides novae***

Dee himself must have felt how intimate they were, and his attempts at excision, conflagration and concealment in chimneys are now well known. The rumour, current in Mortlake and elsewhere in the years after his death, that he had buried his manuscripts was sufficiently compelling to cause one person, the antiquary and book collector Sir Robert Cotton (1571-1631), to purchase some of Dee's land. The excavations proved successful and a significant cache of manuscripts came to light.[7] Meric Casaubon, their first editor (1659), takes up the story:

The book had been buried in the earth, how long, years or months, I know not; but so long, though it was carefully kept since, yet it retained so much of the earth, that it began to moulder and perish some years ago, which when Sir Thomas C. (Sir Robert Cotton's son) observed, he was at the charge to have it written out, before it should be too late.[8]

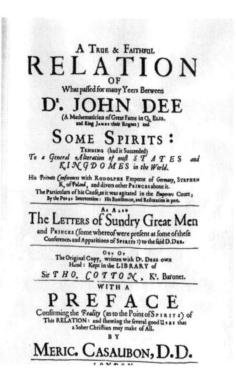

A True & Faithful

RELATION

OF

What passed for many Years Between

D². JOHN DEE

(A Mathematician of Great Fame in Q. Eliz.
and King James their Reigns) and

SOME SPIRITS:

Tending (had it Succeeded)
To a *General Alteration of most STATES and KINGDOMES in the World.*

His *Private Conferences* with RODOLPHE Emperor of *Germany*, STEPHEN K. of *Poland*, and divers other PRINCES about it.
The Particulars of his Cause, as it was agitated in the *Emperors* Court; By the Popes Intercession: His Banishment, and Restoration in part.

As Also

The LETTERS of Sundry Great Men

and PRINCES (some whereof were present at some of these Conferences and Apparitions of SPIRITS t) to the said D.DEE.

Out Of
The Original Copy, written with D². DEES own Hand: Kept in the LIBRARY of
Sir THO. COTTON, K². Baronet.

WITH A

PREFACE

Confirming the *Reality* (as to the Point of SPIRITS) of This RELATION: and shewing the several good USES that a Sober Christian may make of All.

BY

MERIC. CASAUBON, D.D.

Casaubon was clearly aware of the fragmentary nature of this material but was not optimistic that any further Dee papers would ever be found:

Now full fifty years, or not many wanting, being passed since this original came to Sir Robert, it is very likely, that had any more in all that time been heard of, Sir Robert, or Sir Thomas, his son and heir, would have heard of it, and got it as soon as anybody else: and because no more hath been heard of all this while, it is more than probable that no more is extant, not in England, nor I think anywhere else.

A cedar wood chest that soon afterwards fell into the hands of Elias Ashmole was to prove him wrong. [9]

[1] 'Scryers' used reflective objects (pools of water, mirrors, crystals, stones) to find lost items, see into the future or make contact with spirits.

[2] The Greek delta is Dee's shorthand for his own name.

[3] Robert Cecil (1563-1612), Earl of Salisbury, son of William Cecil, Queen Elizabeth's chief secretary of state, who himself became secretary of state in 1596.

[4] The young man would presumably have been one of Dee's servants. John Pontoys (1565-1624) was a London merchant with interests in both Poland and the New World. He seems to have been the close companion of Dee's final years. He was also Dee's executor (although no will was ever found) and custodian of the Mortlake Library.

[5] Pawned for £5 in January 1601 and never redeemed. A sign, surely, of Dee's confusion in his old age.

[6] Dee's anxiety about this would have been well known to Hickman. The house had been first left empty in 1583 when Dee moved his family and household to Poland. On that occasion the building, with its library and contents, was broken into. A second occasion was when Dee left Mortlake to take up the Wardenship of Christ's College, Manchester, in 1596.

[7] Charles Hailstone records in *Alleyways of Mortlake and East Sheen* (see entry on Church Path) the discovery between the wars of a possible Dee relic in the back garden of No.94 Mortlake High Street (now part of the site of John Dee House). This was 'a large stone globe, whereabouts now unknown, full of glittering crystal when broken open.'

[8] *A True and Faithful Relation of What Passed for Many Years Between Dr John Dee and Some Spirits.*

[9] See Epilogue for more of the story.

Chapter 1

A Brief Life of Dr John Dee

Birth
London 13 July 1527

The facts surrounding Dee's birth could not be clearer, although no parish record of it exists.[10] *Bodleian MS Ashmole 1788* is a collection of Dee manuscripts in Oxford, among which is a small and apparently insignificant square piece of paper. This paper is the horoscope of John Dee, created by Dee himself, in the traditional form of a square containing a handwritten record of the date and location of his birth. This square is in turn set within a diamond, the triangular segments of which contain additional information and the ascendant houses of the Zodiac.

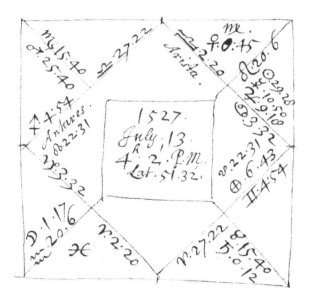

From this we learn that John Dee first saw the light of day at 4.02 on the afternoon of 13 July 1527, at a point 51 degrees and 32 minutes north of the Equator. This conveniently is the latitude of the City of London, although modern measurement might put this point more accurately just north of London Wall. The longitude of Dee's nativity, however, presents a greater problem, for there was no meridian in existence at the time, and even if there had been there was not the accurate measurement to make proper use of it. Yet it is possible from the position of the sun in the horoscope to make an informed guess: this reassuringly turns out to be a few miles from the later Greenwich meridian, in the Tower Ward of the City of London just west of the Tower itself. This means that the parish record of John Dee's birth, if it had ever existed, would have been found in the church of St Dunstan-in-the-East in Lower Thames Street.[11]

All this tallies with the known whereabouts of Dee's father, Rowland Dee, a textile merchant, and from 1526 a member of the Mercers' Company (which Dee joined by patrimony). At the time of his son's birth, however, it seems that Rowland Dee was chiefly in the King's service at Greenwich Palace.[12] *Artessignanus dapiterorum* Dee calls him, in far from Classical Latin – a sort of butler or gentleman 'sewer'[13]. Less clear is Dee's earlier ancestry. That Rowland Dee was a Welshman is certain, that he in turn was the son of Bedo Dee is also certain; beyond that the origins of the Dees become obscure. There was once the general feeling that the family came from Radnorshire; but this was clearly not enough to satisfy Dee, who in later life drew his pedigree in a genealogical roll (British Library, Cotton Charter XIV, article 1), affirming descent from Rhodri Mawr, the 9th century ruler of Wales. He also claimed kinship with King Arthur and the Tudor Queen herself. All this was pure fantasy.

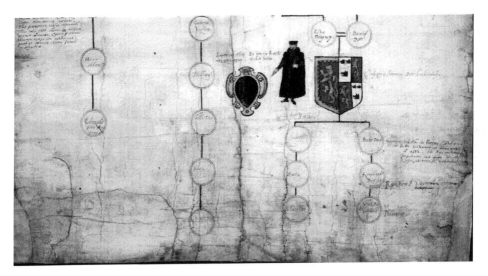

The final section from Dee's genealogical roll showing his lineage and self portrait

18

Education
1534-51

Dee attended Chelmsford Grammar School from the age of seven or eight. In November 1542, aged fifteen, he entered St John's College, Cambridge. There he was an assiduous, even obsessive, scholar:

> *For those years I did inviolably keep this order; only to sleep four hours every day; to allow to meat and drink (and some refreshing after) two hours every day; and of the other eighteen all (except the time of going to and being at divine service) was spent in my studies and learning.*

St John's College, Cambridge

Given this regime, it is hardly surprising that Dee made rapid progress, graduating BA in early 1546 and at the end of that year being appointed Fellow and Under-reader in Greek at the new foundation of Trinity College. Already regarded as a polymath, Dee was duly called upon to employ his mechanical skills in the construction of stage machinery for a college production of Aristophanes' *Peace*. Here the character of Tygaeus was to rise to the heavens (or rather to the rafters of the Great Hall) on the back of a scarab beetle. Dee, the story goes, brought off this stunt so brilliantly that audiences were spellbound and even frightened. From that day onwards Dee's reputation as a practitioner of dark arts and wizardry was to dog him mercilessly and unjustly.

In 1548 he proceeded to the degree of MA and left Cambridge, never to return. This decision was probably his and his alone, based solely on his need to pursue private enthusiasms and independent studies.[14] Had Dee remained in a university fellowship, the financial worries that plagued so much of his life would have been fewer, and his search for that most elusive of persons, the private patron, far less frustrating.

A period of foreign travel came next, during which Dee visited the great universities of Louvain and Antwerp.[15] He was in Paris by July 1550, where, thanks to an already growing continental reputation, he was in great demand as a lecturer:

> I read freely and publicly Euclid's Geometricall, Mathematice, Physice and Pythagorice: a thing never done publicly in any University in Christendom. My auditory was so great and the most part elder than myself, that the mathematical schools could not hold them.

This of course is Dee's own version of events; but the point that he always enjoyed greater recognition in continental Europe still holds good, or at least did so until quite recently.

Even so, the excitement generated by these foreign lectures seems extraordinary. Perhaps Dee was sailing into dangerous waters with his exposition of an occult theory of number. It should not be forgotten that for all scholars of the mid-16th century, 'Mathematice' was the key to the Universe. Dee was no exception. Mathematics for him was at once pragmatic and mystic, on one level a contribution to the art of navigation, on another a devout seeking out of the mysteries of creation. The latter would have had no immediately sinister implications and was wholly legitimate.

Early Patronage
1551-63

Dee returned to England in 1551 and set about looking for a patron. Powerful and influential Protestant families were in the ascendant and Dee quickly attached himself to William Cecil, later Lord Burghley. Cecil introduced Dee to the young Edward VI, who in due course received from the young scholar two astronomical treatises of the Louvain period, one on celestial globes, the other on the sizes and distances of the heavenly bodies. Both were derivative and showed the influence of Mercator; but they earned Dee a pension of one hundred crowns, exchanged in March 1553 for the benefice of Upton-upon-Severn in Worcestershire. This produced eighty pounds a year, a tidy but not extravagant sum.

Meanwhile, on 28 February 1552, Dee entered the service of William Herbert, Earl of Pembroke, probably combining the roles of tutor and caster of horoscopes. This in turn led to service with John Dudley, Duke of Northumberland, a rising star who as Lord President of the Council had recently ousted the Duke of Somerset as Lord Protector of Edward V1. Once again Dee was employed as a tutor – perhaps even as an advisor – and it seems certain that one of his young charges would have been Dudley's fifth son, Robert, later Earl of Leicester and favourite of Elizabeth I. All therefore was set fair for Dee's future career. John Bale for example described him in his *Index Britanniae scriptorum* as an expert astronomer *(astronomus peritissimus)*. Dee's position in the new Protestant order of England indeed seemed secure. Then, in July 1553, the young king died, followed by Northumberland's abortive and ultimately fatal attempt to crown Lady Jane Grey.

Dee's Marian period was not at first an easy one. That he was asked to cast the nativities of their Catholic majesties Philip and Mary boded well; that he also produced a horoscope for the Princess Elizabeth, hope of all disaffected Protestants, did not. He was soon arrested for 'lewd and vain practises of calculing and conjuring', charges that he ably defended. Unfortunately things did not stop there. Amid lingering suspicions of heresy Dee was brought before Edmund Bonner, the 'bloody' Bishop of London and a heartless executor of Mary's religious policies, and duly deprived of the Upton benefice. Dee again acquitted himself well, even to the extent of impressing Bonner as an orthodox Catholic reliable and useful enough to attend the interrogations of others. This all too easily explains the bad press that Dee subsequently received in the first edition of Foxe's *Acts and Monuments of the English Martyrs*, where he is called a 'great conjuror' and identified as the Bishop's private chaplain. These references were removed in the later 1576 edition, but the mud still stuck.

It is at first all too easy to regard Dee as a 16th century Vicar of Bray, a fair-weather placeman without religious principles, driven only by low expediency and the need for self-preservation. Dee was certainly no extremist: there were others of that kind on both sides of the religious divide in Reformation England – often men of high principle who actively courted martyrdom – but they were hardly representative, and Dee was not among them. Modern historiography now suggests that the religion of the English in the 16th century was often more ambivalent, flexible even, than previously realised, and Dee seems to support this view. The evidence of his Mortlake Library certainly suggests that he had little interest in tomes of theology and religious controversy, hence his lifelong refusal to commit himself one way or the other doctrinally. He was certainly no papist or recusant, and indeed was later viewed by the exiled and somewhat militant Cardinal Allen as a suspicious figure given to magic and uncanny arts. Yet all the while he had links with known papists and even advised on the foundation of a Catholic colony in the New World.

The diaries certainly suggest that Dee was pious and not a sectarian, given instead to private prayer and fervent supplication. Above all he believed that God's truth was to be glimpsed in Nature and gained through systematic learning. Later, he believed that angels could bring enlightenment. As a scholar and antiquary, Dee was also drawn to the integrity and unity of the Primitive Church. His religion, in the words of the Dee scholar, Benjamin Woolley, being 'founded on ancient principles and confirmed by science'. The numinous and the scientific were yet as one.

It was also during Mary's reign that Dee emerged as the custodian of Britain's past. The effect of the dissolution of the monasteries had been catastrophic, and Dee was quicker than most to grasp this.[16] The dispersal and destruction of medieval libraries in particular concerned him. In 1556 he addressed a supplication to the Queen 'for the recovery and preservation of ancient writers and monuments' and moved for the foundation of a national library. Nothing of course came of it and Dee was left to rescue manuscripts as best he could. It is also thought that Dee began to read widely in alchemy at this time. He became involved in navigation too, even inventing a *paradoxall compass* for the Muscovy Company.

The reign of Elizabeth promised to repair Dee's fortunes. William Cecil and Dudley had regained their influence and the new Queen was well disposed. His earlier presence in the Bonner household was not now an issue, suggesting that his connection all along had been in the Protestant interest. It also explains why, after the loss of Upton-on-Severn, he was given the Lincolnshire benefice of Leadenham. Next, at the request of Robert Dudley, his former pupil, Dee set about writing a detailed examination of the astrological prospects of the new reign. He chose 15 January 1559 as the auspicious day for its formal inception. Almost certainly, Dee would have been present at Westminster Abbey for the Coronation, tucked away as a commoner at the back of the congregation.

Other than dedicating a second edition of his astronomical work *Propaedeumata Aphoristica* to the Queen, Dee is a somewhat shadowy figure during the early 1560s. The absence of any record in his native land suggests that he was abroad collecting the books and manuscripts that would eventually lay the foundations of the *Bibliotheca Mortlacensis*. It is also likely that he was studying the part-mystical, part-mathematical Cabala, an undertaking that would certainly have required some grounding in Hebrew. It was perhaps from these studies that Dee came to recognise the power of incantation and code.

Frontispiece of Dee's *Monas Hieroglyphica*

Foreign Travel and the 'Monas Hieroglyphica'
1563-4

By February 1563 Dee was certainly in Antwerp and exploring that city's thriving book trade. A very rare manuscript of the *Steganographica* of Trithemius (1462-1516) was soon located, a work full of mystic numerology and complex cryptology.[17] For the sum of twenty pounds, his entire travelling budget, Dee secured the loan of the manuscript and began frantically the arduous task of transcription. Exhausted and penniless, he contacted Cecil in London, reporting the discovery of 'this most precious jewel' and seeking to recover his costs. This would have been wishful thinking, for the pragmatic and conservative Cecil would have had little time for the complex rituals and methodology of the obscure German monk. A workable code might have been an altogether different matter. Yet Dee's presence on the Continent as an 'intelligencer', a seeker-out of knowledge doubling as a spy, was clearly in the interests of the Elizabethan establishment, and was at least tolerated, although never actually rewarded.

After further travel taking in Zürich, Pressburg (Bratislava), Padua, Venice, Urbino and Rome, Dee was back in England by 14 June 1564, when at Greenwich Palace he presented to the Queen a copy of his *Monas Hieroglyphica* printed that same year by Gulielmus Silvius of Antwerp. Such a public gesture was risky in conservative England where Dee's reputation for 'calculing' was still arousing suspicion. This explains the book's actual dedication to the new Holy Roman Emperor, Maximillian II, whose coronation at Pressburg Dee had attended in September 1563. Yet it says much for the young Queen's character and intellect that her response to such modern continental thinking on cosmology and numerology was as positive as it was. The reception granted by English academia was not. Dee was later to write in *A Compendious Rehearsall*: 'University Graduates of high degree dispraised it, because they understood it not'.

The 'Monas' itself is of course none other than Dee's famous hieroglyph:

Monas Hieroglyphica, like the earlier *Propaedeumata Aphoristica*, posits a series of theorems. But whereas the earlier work on astronomy was grounded on empirical observation, the *Monas* is abstract and intuitive, and makes the assumption that the common astronomical symbols have an 'immortal life' and are the relics of a lost universal language transcending religious barriers. Here, perhaps, is the beginning of Dee's 'cosmopolitical' theory, through which he arrived at the concept of a 'Citizen and Member of the whole and only one Mystical City Universal'.[18]

The *Monas* effectively closed the doors of academic advancement on Dee, now already in his mid-thirties. The other and indeed only alternative was the Court. Here, perhaps with some justification, Dee felt that he enjoyed a special relationship with the Tudor Queen. Certainly he was one of the few commoners ever to be honoured with personal visits and was often summoned to Court on various matters. His devotion to Elizabeth was unconditional, even though the 'noble' (either the golden coin or noble title) that she promised him at the beginning of her reign never materialised. Even so, the anticipation of imminent mystical or alchemical revelations must always have attracted Elizabeth to Dee, and he in turn would have been flattered by her interest. But he was not an experienced courtier and seemed rather to believe that cultivating the Queen's servants would produce the desired results, even making a great point of welcoming Elizabeth's Italian dwarf Tomasina to Mortlake in the summer of 1580. His hope that the Queen herself would create the post of court philosopher expressly for him was also wide of the mark for 16th century England.

Marriages and Mortlake
London c.1565/6 – Mortlake 1580

More credible than Dee's descent from King Arthur is the possibility that he might have had Surrey and even Mortlake blood. His mother was a member of the Wild family, and it was doubtless through this connection that she came to be in possession of land and houses in Mortlake. Whether these were deep local roots it is difficult to say. We can be certain, however, that Dee settled permanently in this pleasant and convenient riverside location sometime between the summer of 1564, when he returned from Antwerp and presented *Monas Hieroglyphica* to the Queen, and 18 September 1566 when he inscribed his own copy of the *Monas* thus:[19]

> *'Joannes Dee Londinensis: 1566*
> *Mortlaci Septembris 18'*

It is highly likely that Dee moved to his mother's house as an economy measure. Expected preferment, in the form of the deanery of Gloucester, had not materialised, and there was a further incentive: marriage. It is likely that Dee began married life in the mid-1560s.

Richmond Palace

Of Dee's first wife, Katherine Constable, nothing is known, other than that she was the widow of a London grocer and that she produced no children. Her death in Mortlake, however, is recorded by Dee as having taken place on 10 March 1575, the day he also received a visit from the Queen herself on her way from Richmond to London:[20]

My wife was within four hours buried out of the house, her Majesty refused to come in; but willed me to fetch my glass so famous and to show unto her some of the properties of it, which I did; her Majesty being taken down from her horse by the Earle of Leicester, Master of the horse, by the Church wall of Mortlack, did see some of the properties of that glass, to her Majesties great contentment and delight, and so in most gracious manner did thank me.

The reference here to the Mortlake church wall is interesting and, as we shall see in a later chapter, helps fix the boundary of the Dee property. The advantageous location of the house is also confirmed: hence the steady stream of illustrious visitors, foreign dignitaries and courtiers who dropped in, by river or by road, on their way to Richmond and Hampton Court from the City of London or the royal palaces of Westminster and Greenwich. Nearby was also Barn Elms, the country seat of Sir Francis Walsingham, Elizabeth's spymaster, and from 1573 her chief Secretary of State.

Dee remained a widower for less than three years, becoming betrothed to Jane Fromond of Cheam on 5 January 1578 and marrying her on 5 February.[21] She was twenty-two years of age: Dee at fifty was twenty-eight years her senior. Perhaps it was this marriage and the immediate prospect of fatherhood, as well as his mother's increasing age, that led to the house being surrendered to Dee and his heirs in 1579.[22] When therefore his mother died in October 1580, Dee at once took possession by due process of law.

Navigation and Government Work
1569-82

Slowly the 'house of natural philosophy' with its great *Bibliotheca externa*, its annexes and laboratories, took shape. It required beyond all doubt an outlay well beyond the £80 that Dee was receiving annually from the rectory of Leadenham. To finance his projects Dee therefore turned to tutoring, astrology, dream interpretation and even medical practice. The diaries contain some tantalising glimpses of the sad cases seeking treatment from Doctor Dee. Who for example was Isabel Lister, a local woman with a collection of knives who had so far resisted suicide? Or the destitute woman, led by a dream, who had been digging compulsively for buried treasure? There is also the sinister Charles Sled whose two massive nosebleeds, according to the spirit Galvah, signified the successful exorcism of an evil spirit.[23] And who was the unfortunate William Rogers of Mortlake who cut his throat at seven o'clock in the morning on 3 November 1577?

Meanwhile, there was government work to be done, including a commission to write an analysis of the state of the British nation. The result, *Brytanniae Reipublicae Synopsis*, is regarded by historians of Elizabethan England as an important contemporary survey of the nation's political institutions, defences and moribund economy. No record remains of what fee, if any, Dee received. Later, it was certainly his custom to refuse payment for such work. Dee's interest in alchemy was also proceeding apace, and in 1571 he was given a passport to travel to the Duchy of Lorraine to purchase equipment and materials. A subsequent illness is thought by some to have been caused by chemical poisoning associated with alchemical practice.

In 1574 Dee petitioned William Cecil for financial assistance, at the same time suggesting the possibility of locating buried treasure as a means of repayment. Cecil demurred, reluctant to grant Dee a monopoly at odds with the Crown's treasure-trove policy. Dee next turned to navigation and the untold riches promised by the Orient and the New World. In the early 1550s he had already prepared accurate charts for Richard Chancellor, whose later unsuccessful attempt to establish a north-east passage to China via the coast of Russia was to lead to contact with the court of Ivan the Terrible and the foundation of the Muscovy Company.

It is at this point that the dynamic figure of Martin Frobisher bursts upon the scene and with him the grandiose notion of discovering an alternative route to China – one that was to exercise British seamen for decades – the fabled Northwest Passage. In this he was inspired by Humphrey Gilbert, who in turn might have been encouraged by Dee's own work on the subject. Frobisher accordingly set out to test Gilbert's theory, overcoming the inevitable hostility of the Muscovy Company and making preparations for the voyage. The 'Company of Kathai' was duly formed and Dee brought in to 'examine and instruct' the expedition's leaders, Frobisher himself and Hall, both of whom as practical seamen were mathematically challenged. Dee did what he could in the space of just one month, and on 7 June 1576 the *Michael* and the *Gabriel* left Deptford for the open seas. After extraordinary adventures and privations, the expedition reached Greenland and north-east Canada; but on its return, some two years later, the Northwest Passage remained as hidden as ever.[24] The only trophies to reach England were a strange lustrous black stone and an Inuk (or 'Eskimo'). Later

Frobisher expeditions were to bring back large quantities of this stone, which to his great chagrin yielded only infinitesimal and uneconomical amounts of gold and silver. The Cathay Company eventually went into receivership. Dee probably lost money.

Frontispiece of Dee's *General and Rare Memorials,* 1577

It was also at this time that Dee made an extraordinary proposal to the Queen concerning her dominions: that as the lineal successor of King Arthur she should lay claim to the New World and challenge the Treaty of Tordesillas (1494), Pope Alexander VI's division of the Americas in favour of Spain and Portugal. The groundwork for this was Dee's monumental manuscript opus, the four-volume

General and Rare Memorials Pertaining to the Perfect Art of Navigation. Volumes II and III have been lost, and what remains of Volume IV, *Of Famous and Rich Discoveries*, is badly burnt; but Volume I survives both in manuscript and in a number of printed copies. It also features a wonderful allegorical title page celebrating the sea power of Elizabethan England and a proposal within setting out the construction of a great navy. The work is at once practical and mystical, political and scholarly. In it, as in the much shorter *Brytanici Imperii Limites* (*The Limits of the British Empire*), Dee effectively lays the foundations of a British identity that would in time go far beyond the shores of a small island kingdom. The Mortlake house soon became an important centre for navigators and privateers, two of whom, Adrian Gilbert and John Davis (who would later help himself to books from Dee's library), were particularly regular visitors. It was Gilbert who would later promise Dee in perpetuity all 'royalties of discoveries' north of the 50th Parallel – in other words the whole of Alaska and most of Canada.

Dee's alchemical endeavours were renewed in the early months of 1580, and on 17 September he was again visited by the Queen, who at once commanded his presence at Richmond Palace. There can be no doubt that she was excited by Dee's work on her title to the New World, although her chief minister, the ever-cautious Cecil, was lukewarm and wary of upsetting the Spaniards. He and Dee then fell out, despite the former's peace offering of a haunch of venison, which perhaps explains Dee's subsequent withdrawal from grandiose political schemes and the court itself. In any case, his career was soon to take another direction.

Angelic Actions: Edward Kelley
1582-3

There is some evidence that Dee had already contacted spirits through the use of crystals, perhaps even as early as 1568.[25] But the first explicit reference in the diary is to 22 June 1579, when the Hickman brothers, Richard and Bartholomew, came to Mortlake. In May 1581 Dee himself had 'sight *in Chrystallō*' but found to his great disappointment that he had no gift as a medium and would have to rely henceforth on an adept. His first full-time scryer, Barnabas Saul, soon proved unsatisfactory, and later fraudulent. So it was at a critical point that the infamous Edward 'Talbot' arrived at Mortlake, in the company of Mr Clerkson, an agent in matters alchemical and occult. Later that day Dee, a great watcher of the heavens, a tracker of comets and student of the portentous 1572 nova in Cassiopeia, would see the night sky over Mortlake all blood-red and fiery. Perhaps here was an omen. Talbot returned the next day to Mortlake – alone.

Edward Kelley

Talbot – but Kelley seems to have been his real name if we trace his roots to his native Worcester – was a low-born and half-educated misfit with a criminal past, a kind not uncharacteristic of late 16th century vagabondage. The cowl he wore gave him a monkish and erudite appearance, and it is just possible that he was a Roman Catholic priest who had lost, or been deprived of, his vocation. It is possible too that he was mentally ill, if not mad. His arrival at Mortlake, of all places, is probably explained by his being a fugitive who simply wished to lie low and make use of convenient cover. Perhaps he at once saw the possibility of rich pickings and formed new plans. Whatever his motive, he set about making himself indispensable to Dee, and was soon offering him a direct line to Enoch and the pre-lapsarian Adamic language that this ancient seer had recorded. Next followed enlightenment from the angel Uriel regarding the reliability of Dee's manuscript copy of *The Book of Soyga*. There was also guidance on the construction of a 'Table of Practice' to be used in subsequent spirit conversations, and a glimpse in the show stone of a chair to be called the 'seat of perfection'. At once the Archangel Michael appeared seated on it, sword in hand, and a kneeling figure at his feet, robed in silk and crowned with laurel, whom he knighted with the sword. The unknown person then stood up and turned, as if looking out of the stone, and revealed himself as Dee. Everything now was wonderfully clear: full recognition and consecration by God's angels had come.

John Dee a detail from the frontispiece of Meric Casaubon's
A True and Faithful Relation

Further revelations from Michael followed, chiefly focussed on the link between divine and temporal power, and also an injunction that Talbot should marry.[26] At this point, Dee's relations with his scryer turned sour, and Jane Dee, exasperated no doubt by the developing situation, lost her temper. Talbot, also in high dudgeon, left the house; whereupon the discredited Barnabas Saul, seizing at once the opportunity, sought reinstatement but was given short shrift. Months passed. When finally Talbot reappeared in November, now under the name of Kelley, the welcome was different. This seems extraordinary today; but it should be realised that Kelley's volatility, unreliability and mystery were precisely the psychological qualities that made him appear such a gifted medium in the eyes of a devout 16th century natural philosopher. Yet it would be doing Dee an injustice to suggest that he was completely gullible and unaware of Kelley's criminal inclinations. The simple fact is that the brilliance and sophistication of Kelley's visions, as well as his apparent mastery of humanist learning and cabalistic formulae, were all as convincing as they were compelling. If, as seems certain, Kelley was a fraud, he was a very good one: a conman who knew precisely what Dee wanted to hear. Besides, the possibility that he was completely or in part delusional – in other words mentally ill – should not be dismissed. At the very least he was highly intelligent and an extraordinarily creative allegorist.

The first 'Action' after the reconciliation took place on 21 November 1582, during which a spirit called King Camara gave Dee a new magical lens. Immediately afterwards Dee had a nightmare in which he saw himself dead and his books scrutinized by a sour-looking Cecil. Kelley then left Mortlake, ostensibly to visit Oxfordshire. All spirit conversation ceased. Time passed. In March of the following year Kelley returned with a treasure map, a red powder said to transmute base matter into gold, and a wife.[27] The renewed angelic actions, not surprisingly, were once again inconclusive and obscure, with Kelley's creation of the elaborately allegorical 'Medicina Dei' and pascal lamb featuring prominently.

It was also at this time, on a rather more terrestrial footing, that Dee became involved in the reform of the calendar. On 24 February 1582 the papal bull *Inter gravissimas* of Gregory XIII had reformed the Julian calendar, the main effect being a loss of ten days. Dee was consulted and on 26 February 1583 delivered to Cecil his *Plain discourse as concerning the needful reformation of the vulgar calendar*, recommending the removal of, not ten, but eleven days. The adoption of the new Roman calendar, though acceptable to civil government, came in the end to nothing, being blocked by Archbishop Grindal and the entire Convocation of Anglican Bishops.[28]

Dee's continuing sessions with Kelley must have soon become known, at least in part, to some of his contemporaries, of whom a number, doubtless, sought angelic advice. But very few, if any, would have known that Dee was taking down, via Kelley's dictation, *The Book of Enoch* in its original Adamic language against a forty-day deadline. Meanwhile, Dee's fame as an alchemist and occultist had spread to Europe, possibly through the influence of Sir Philip Sidney. It is this which is the most plausible explanation for the visit of the Polish nobleman Albrecht Łaski, Palatine of Sieradz, to Mortlake.

Łaski arrived in England on 1 May 1583 and met Dee some twelve days later in the Earl of Leicester's apartments at Greenwich Palace before finally visiting Mortlake on 18 May. A month later, Łaski reappeared but this time on the river in the Queen's barge, in the company of Sidney and Lord Russell. There is every indication that this Polish nobleman was being wooed by the Protestant party as a possible player against Catholic and Hapsburg interests in central Europe. And Łaski, for his part, might have had designs on the elective crown of Poland, advancing himself politically and financially (through alchemy?) as a logical successor to Stefan Batory. What is certainly clear is that Łaski was soon joining Dee and Kelley in their angelic actions at Mortlake. The evidence also points to the possibility that Łaski's entertainment was being subsidised by the Queen herself. There is also some suggestion that Dee's subsequent proposed journey with Łaski to Poland was viewed favourably and expedited. Even so, Dee's leaving behind the greater part of his library, his neglect of the Northwest Passage, and the mortgage arrangement he entered into with his brother-in-law (to raise £400 travelling money on the Mortlake house), were to have long-term consequences.

Poland and Bohemia
1583-9

Dee left Mortlake on 21 September 1583 with his wife Jane and three children (Arthur b.1579, Katherine b.1581 and Roland b.1583). There was also Kelley, his wife Joanna (or Joan) and perhaps her two children from an earlier marriage. A retinue of servants and eight hundred books brought up the rear. The party moved first to Greenwich and then to beyond Gravesend, where they boarded ship. The journey by sea was difficult, the journey by land across north Germany in the snows of winter even more painfully slow. Some three months later, on Christmas Day, they arrived at Szczecin (Stettin) on the Baltic coast. Sieradz (Łasko) itself, in central-western Poland, was not reached until February 1584. But angelic actions continued and were soon a feature of life there and later at Kraków. Dee's intention, it seems, was to remain in Poland for no more than a year, especially once contact with Łaski himself became infrequent.

RVDOLPHVS II. D. G. ROM. IMPERAT.
SEMPER AVG.GERMAN.HVNG.BOHEM.
&c.REX,ARCHID.AVSTR.DVX BVRG.&c.
Anton.Wiern fecit et excud.

Rudolph II

Things being moribund, Dee and Kelley followed the advice of the angels and set out for Prague. Here, letters from England sent out in April informed Dee that his house and library had been broken into. This was a worrying development. Stirred into action, Dee secured a brief and unproductive interview with Rudolf II on 3 September 1584, soon followed by a claim that he could produce the philosopher's stone. Yet the Emperor was unmoved. In April 1585 the disappointed English party returned to Kraków, where Łaski was able to introduce Dee to Stefan Batory as an alternative patron. This too proved unsuccessful. A return to Prague became inevitable, together with renewed and ever more desperate 'angelic' activity.

In May 1586 Dee met a better prospect, the Bohemian nobleman Vilém Rožmberk, who seems to have stimulated in Dee a renewed interest in alchemy. But disaster struck at the end of the month: Dee and Kelley, at the instance of the Papal Nuncio, were banished from the domains of the Holy Roman Emperor. Books found in their possession were burnt in Prague and the future began to look ominous. Fortunately, Rožmberk came to the rescue and sought leave for the pair and their dependants to remain on his estate at Třeboň. This they finally reached in September 1586.

Prague in the early seventeenth century

Here, the alchemy continued but with Kelley increasingly in the ascendant. This perhaps explains why Dee, when the Angelic Actions were resumed, sought to develop the scrying role of his seven year old son, Arthur. The final recorded actions with Kelley took place in April 1587, during which Kelley received from the spirit Madimi the doctrine of 'cross-matching', duly consummated towards the end of May.[29] Thanks to the patronage of Rožmberk, Dee must have lived quite comfortably at Třeboň; but by November 1588 he was making plans to return home. He bequeathed to Kelley his alchemical apparatus and materials. The two men parted on 16 February 1589, Kelley riding out just after midday in the direction of Prague, never to be seen again.

Kelley remained in Bohemia, but his star began to fall. It is possible that he was first a mercenary in the war against the Turks – Dee for one certainly believed that he had been killed in action in 1595 – but it has now been established by the Czech scholar Ivan Sviták that Kelley was still alive in 1596, imprisoned in a castle in Western Bohemia. At this point legend takes over. One tradition has it

36

that he escaped; another that he faked his own suicide. It is even possible that he ended up in Russia as an alchemist, although the last sighting of him was back in Bohemia in 1598. After that he simply vanishes into the mists of time, as mysteriously as he came.

Dee's own preparations now proceeded apace, and on 11 March he too left Třeboň with his family and possessions in three great wagons, eventually reaching England on 23 November 1589.

The Return to England and Manchester
1589-1605

On his return Dee's most pressing business was to recover his pilfered books and secure an income to support his growing family (Michael b.1585, Theodore b.1588, Madimia b.1590, Frances b.1592 and Margaret b.1595). This took time and was not easy, let alone successful; but he finally came to a financial accommodation of some kind with his brother-in-law and recovered part of the missing library. Having through neglect of a legal point lost his income from the church living of Leadenham, Dee relied on grants, loans, occasional fees and pawning. He also petitioned the Queen for relief and penned his *Compendious Rehearsall*, gaining for his family some measure of financial assistance, but for himself no preferment worthy of his intellectual accomplishments and prestige. In May 1595 Dee was finally given the wardenship of the collegiate foundation of Manchester parish church, taking up his duties in February 1596. He doubtless did so half-heartedly. The years had brought disappointments and regrets, while his present difficulties perhaps suggested that he had somehow implicated himself in the atheistic 'School of Night' of Sir Walter Raleigh and Henry Percy, the 'Wizard Earl' of Northumberland. It is almost certain that Dee would have met the playwright and poet Christopher Marlowe through the complex networks of Raleigh and Percy patronage, and perhaps he knew the men themselves through meetings at Durham House, the Earl's London residence, or Syon House. There is certainly a record of Dee having dined privately with Sir Walter Raleigh.

Many of Dee's generation were now in advanced age or else dead. The Earl of Leicester, Sidney and Walsingham were no more. William Cecil, perhaps the nearest thing to a patron Dee ever had, was now an old man, and his son Robert was stepping into his shoes. The Queen herself was ageing. Dee too began to feel the weight of the years, suffering from the kidney stones already mentioned and for which he took 'a draught of white wine and salet oil and after crab's eyes in powder with the bone of a carp's head'.

Manchester College in the late eighteenth century

His time in Manchester was not a happy one. With his reputation doubtless preceding him, and viewed as a southern interloper, Dee was not well received. The affairs of the college were also in some disarray, and the fellows, notably one Oliver Carter, touchy and defensive. There was little time for private study. The dismemberment of late medieval England throughout four successive Tudor reigns had left many knotty legal problems, and Manchester was no exception. A great deal of administrative work involving land, property and boundaries needed to be done on behalf of the college. There was also the vexed question of Dee's canonical status. In all his professional life he had never undertaken priestly duties, and this in turn had necessitated the appointment (and payment) of various curates. But there was at least the visit of the great cartographer Christopher Saxton to Manchester in 1596 by way of compensation, and the important survey of the city that followed in 1597. In the same year, Dee appeared as an expert witness in the case of demonic possession known as the 'Seven in Lancashire'. He also published in September 1597, at the request of Sir Edward Dyer, *Thalattokratia Brettanike*, a discussion of British sea power and his last maritime tract. Dee is famously credited with being the first person to use the phrase 'British Empire'.

The famines of the 1590s must have had a dire effect on the Dee household. Welsh cousins sent cattle to Manchester, and John Pontoys, the Baltic merchant who was to be the friend of Dee's declining years, offered a consignment of Danish rye. Between March 1598 and June 1600 Dee was probably in London, ostensibly on college business. In August 1600 he visited Manchester Grammar School and to his 'great grief' discovered 'great imperfection in all and every of

38

the scholars'.[30] Then on 29 September, in front of witnesses, he burnt all records of the angelic visions of Bartholomew Hickman; but strangely, while Dee was distancing himself from his old scryer, the irascible Roger Cook, the alchemist from the first Mortlake period, appeared with an uncharacteristically 'gentle offer and promise'. Such a return to alchemical dreams, if this is what Cook's presence signified, possibly confirms Dee's deepening poverty. There is certainly evidence that he was forced to borrow money from Edward Chetham in Manchester and to pawn his own plate.

It is roughly at this point, on 6 April 1601, that the diary breaks off and we encounter increasing difficulty piecing together the last years of Dee's life. Theodore, the child of the 'cross-matching'[31] pact at Třebon, seems to have died just days after the last entry, following the sickly Michael (d.1594) and possibly Frances (d.1595/6?).[32] The old Queen herself died in 1603 and on the accession of James I, Dee claimed to be the Stuart monarch's 'sworn servant'.

The new King's reputation as a seeker-out of witchcraft must have unsettled him, for in June 1604 Dee commissioned the printing of a petition to the King, to which were attached verses addressed to the Commons denying slanderous rumours of conjuring. He was probably in London during this sensitive period (1604/5) and seems therefore to have escaped the plague that devastated Manchester in the spring of 1605 and took away all the members of his immediate family apart from the two eldest, Arthur (now 25) and Katherine (now 23). The record survives in Manchester of Jane Dee's burial on 23 March 1605, aged fifty; but of the younger children, Roland (aged 22), Madimia (aged 15) and Margaret (aged 9) there is none. As there is no later record of them either, we have to conclude that they too succumbed.

A LETTER,

Containing a moſt briefe Diſcourſe Apo-
logeticall, with a plaine Demonſtration, and feruent
Proteſtation, for the lawfull, ſincere, very faithfull and
Chriſtian courſe, of the Philoſophicall ſtudies and exerci-
ſes, of a certaine ſtudious Gentleman: An ancient
Seruaunt to her moſt excellent
Maieſty Royall.

Dee's 1604 Petition to the King

40

Old Age
1605-8

In the aftermath of this tragedy, Dee probably returned to Mortlake. He was now seventy-seven. His daughter Katherine, we know, was with him from then on, but his son Arthur, who had married in 1602, had responsibilities of his own.[33] The summer of 1607 saw the resumption of angelic conversations at various locations in London and then back in Mortlake, with Bartholomew Hickman again in favour after many years of absence. This seems an extraordinary development, given Dee's recent burning of papers and records. A second journey into Europe was now proposed by the spirits, but nothing came of it. The last coherent entry in the Spiritual Diary is 7 September 1608, but it is uncertain now whether Dee is in London or in Mortlake. What is clear is that Dee's friend John Pontoys has arrived (to join Hickman or to save Dee from his clutches?) and is anxious to know, via the Archangel Raphael, whether he will be thought fit to serve Dr Dee after Hickman's departure. It is also possible that Dee, who was increasingly infirm, was moved at this time to Pontoys' house in Bishopsgate.

It is tempting to think that Pontoys, whose chief interest in life seems to have been the making of money, was in league with Hickman; but it is difficult to imagine a well connected Baltic merchant, who was later vice-admiral of the Virginia Company and its representative on the privy council, stooping quite so low. Besides, there is no clear evidence against Hickman either. It is more likely that Pontoys was convinced of Dee's value as an alchemist and searcher-out of buried treasure and was eager to attract the old man's goodwill and assistance during his declining years. Indeed the evidence of the very last 'angel conversations' suggests that Pontoys too was under the influence of the spirits and wanted to know both the identity of his own 'proper angel' and whether he too might become a scryer. He would also have held Dee's contributions to the science of navigation in high regard and might even have had Polish connections and experiences in common. It is perfectly reasonable to assume that Pontoys moved Dee into his London house out of kindness so that the old man might be more comfortable and better cared for as his life ebbed slowly away in the final months of 1608.

[10] This is not surprising. Dee was a pre-Elizabethan. His birth was even before 1538, the year when keeping parish records became official. There were further initiatives in 1558 and 1597, at the beginning and end of Elizabeth's reign respectively, to enforce the keeping of more accurate records.

[11] Built in 1382, rebuilt by Christopher Wren in 1668, and severely gutted during enemy action in 1941. Only the tower is preserved. The parish records of St Dunstan-in-the-East begin, not surprisingly, with the year 1558.

[12] Greenwich is therefore another possible birthplace, especially if one allows for a minor error in the co-ordinates of the horoscope.

[13] A 'sewer' was an important court servant, responsible for seating arrangements, table setting and service during ceremonial dining.

[14] Dee was later, according the account he gave of his own career in *A Compendious Rehearsall*, to turn down offers from both Oxford and the University of Paris.

[15] If Dee ever possessed a genuine doctorate, it is likely to have been granted by the University of Louvain.

[16] Interestingly, Dee took little part in the programme initiated by Archbishop Parker for the recovery of Early English and especially Anglo-Saxon manuscripts. His chief interest seems to have been in British (ie Celtic) antiquities. The pride he took in his Welsh ancestry probably explains this.

[17] It is unclear whether Dee at the time realised that the mystical *Steganographica* was also a code book. Interestingly, the code that appears in Book III was only cracked in the 1990s.

[18] John Dee: *General and Rare Memorials Pertaining to the Perfect Art of Navigation* (London, 1577).

[19] This copy of the *Monas* is numbered 2108 in the 1583 Mortlake Library Catalogue. The volume found its way eventually, and after many vicissitudes, to the Hunterian Library, Glasgow, where it now rests.

[20] It is sometimes suggested that Dee married three times (eg Benjamin Woolley *The Queen's Conjuror*, p.130). If this is so, the death of an unknown *second* wife seems likely on this date. This means that the death of Katherine Dee would have been earlier and never recorded.

[21] Dee himself always used the form 'Fromonds'.

[22] The legal process lasted between June and October 1579. Arthur, the Dees' first child, was born in July.

[23] An exorcism carried out by Dee? Charles Sled was a spy in the service of Sir Francis Walsingham. He is credited with having infiltrated the English College in Rome and identifying it as a training ground for missionary priests.

[24] The name Frobisher bestowed on this region over four hundred years ago, *Meta Incognita* (the 'Unknown Limit'), holds good to this day.

[25] A crystal ball that once belonged to Dee and his famous obsidian mirror are now in the British Museum. Dee would have seen himself first and foremost as a student of optics, not as a conjuror of 'divels' (devils).

[26] Talbot at first felt that this was 'contrary' to his 'vow and profession'. This has led to the speculation, already noted, that Kelley was in Catholic orders, or at least wanted Dee to believe that he was. The legends and identities surrounding him are legion.

[27] Joan or Joanna Kelley (née Cooper) of Chipping Norton, Oxon. Born in 1563, she appears to have married in either May or June 1582, at the age of eighteen or nineteen. Kelley left Mortlake for a couple of months in early May – immediately after Jane's eruption of 6 May it would seem – and is thought to have returned to his native Worcester. Chipping Norton was on his route and it is likely that he made, or renewed, the acquaintance of Jane Cooper as he passed through. The marriage was not a happy one. See Chapter 3 as to whether or not Joanna Cooper was a widow with children.

[28] The Gregorian calendar was in the end not adopted until 1752.

[29] See Chapter 3 for a much fuller treatment of this bizarre episode, and in particular how it affected Jane Dee.

[30] Dee's son Roland, now aged 17, might just have been still a pupil at the school.

[31] It is possible that Theodore was the son of Kelley. For a full account of the 'cross-matching' between the Dees and the Kelleys, see Chapter 3.

[32] Frances is not mentioned in the company of her sisters Madimia and Margaret in September 1596, and Dee pawned her godmother's silver christening gift to her the following year.

[33] Arthur Dee (1579-1651) was an alchemist and physician. He was at the court of the Tsar for a number of years and then settled in Norwich. He had twelve children, and it is through him and his own son Roland (1613-87) that the Dee line continued.

Chapter 2

The Mortlake House

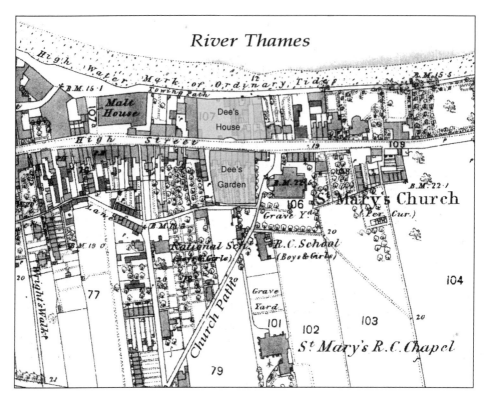

Dee's record of his mother's legal surrender of the Mortlake house survives in the diary:

> 15 June 1579 *My mother surrendered Mortlack houses and land, and had state given in open court until the end of her life: and to me was also the reversion delivered by written contract, and to my wife Jane by me, and after to my heirs and assignees for ever, to understand Mr Bullock: and Mr Taylor, surveyor: at Wimbledon under the tree by the church.* [34]

By 31 October the process of conveyance and inheritance was complete:

> *The fine of 20s paid for my mother's surrender. Paid 20s fine for me and Jane my wife to the Lord of Wimbledon (the Queen), by Goodman Burton*

of Putney: for the surrender taken of my mother, of all she hath in Mortlack: to Jane and me, and then to my heirs and assignees, Etc.

A little less than a year later, on 10 October 1580, Dee's mother was dead, a sad event that coincided with a visit from the Queen:

At 4 of the clock in the morning my mother Jane Dee died at Mortlack. She made a godly end: God be praised therefore. She was 77 year old. The Queen's Majesty, to my great comfort (hora 5), came with her train from the court and at my door, graciously calling me to her, on horseback, exhorted me briefly to take my mother's death patiently . . . She remembered also how at my wife's death it was her fortune likewise to call upon me.

Dee was therefore left in sole possession of the Mortlake house.

It is impossible, after four centuries, to give an accurate account of the house of John Dee. Some of the physical evidence must surely lie buried beneath numbers 77, 99 and 101 Mortlake High Street, the High Street itself, and the block of flats on the south side of the road known as John Dee House; but nothing short of a major archaeological excavation will ever bring anything to light. Numbers 77 and 99 are now the residential riverside developments known as Duke's Court and Tapestry Court, the latter taking its name from Tapestry Green that leads down to the river between it and number 101. This present open space marks the site of the cottage and laboratories that also belonged to Dee. A number of diary entries between May and September 1593 actually record the process of a 16th century property conveyance, in which Dee purchased a house from Mr Mark Perpoint and a 'hovel' from Goodman Welder in an adjoining yard. Perhaps it was these buildings that were purchased in 1619 by Sir Frances Crane, the founder of the Mortlake Tapestry Works, becoming known in due course as the 'Lower Dutch House' from the Flemish weavers who worked on the site. It seems reasonable to assume that Dee's laboratories would have lent themselves to such 'industrial' use and would have required adaptation rather than complete demolition.

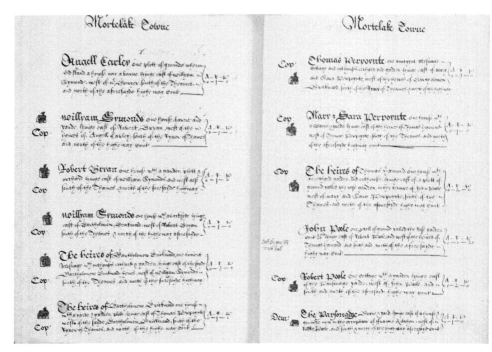

The page from Treswell's 1617 Survey, showing Dee's property

The 1617 survey by Ralph Treswell of the Manor of Wimbledon is the usual and indeed only point of departure.[35] Dee's house is clearly the following property:

1 ancient messuage and cottage and outhouses, orchard and garden lying E of Mary and Sara Perpoynte, W. of the heirs of Bartholomew Brickwood, S. of the River Thames. N. of the Highway.

By 1617 the house itself appears to be the property of Thomas Perpoynte, a local man of some substance in possession of various properties and pockets of land, clearly related to the Mark Perpoint who had sold Dee the cottage in 1593.

There was also the piece of land which, according to John Aubrey, was sold separately to Robert Cotton, and where it was rumoured (correctly as it turned out) that Dee had buried valuable manuscripts. As for Dee himself, there is no reference in the Treswell survey either to him or his immediate surviving family; none to his in-laws the Fromonds, who through the 1583 mortgage might still have had a financial interest in Mortlake; and none to Dee's mother's family (the Wilds). It is as if all connection had ceased. The only other possibility is if we look for a link further back on the female side, through Dee's maternal grandmother, if her maiden name could be established. However, Dee makes no reference in his diaries to any relatives of any name living in Mortlake, although he does mention his cousin, Dr Aubrey, residing at nearby Kew.

The survey is clearly recording the presence of a house of some standing. *Messuage* is an old Anglo-Norman term and means a piece of land on which a dwelling house has been built. There is also the implication that the plot should be large enough to accommodate other buildings. Dee's property, with its orchard, garden, outhouses and cottage (the latter purchased by him to create extra accommodation), certainly conformed to this traditional type. Even if we were not told that it was an 'ancient' place in 1617, there is every indication that a *messuage* in Mortlake High Street would have pre-dated the mid-16th century growth of Mortlake High Street that followed the removal of the Church to its present site.[36] In Treswell's survey there is reference to just one other *messuage* in the immediate area. This house and Dee's were obviously rustic properties from a different century, in all likelihood the 15th ('ancient' in the early 17th century clearly being a relative term).

This evidence gives us some clue as to the likely physical appearance of the house, only these days we have to travel out into rural Surrey, to the Weald and even into Sussex to have some inkling of what it might have been like.

The above drawing of Dee's house, reproduced in Mary Grimwade's *Lesser Houses of East Sheen and Mortlake*[37], suggests a rambling half-timbered place with a large and very steeply pitched roof that might have been originally thatched. The much-loved Alfriston Clergy House in East Sussex owned by the National Trust, springs immediately to mind. Current thinking suggests that this was the residence of a well-to-do farmer, not a priest, and this would tally nicely with the Dee residence in its original state. Built in the mid-14th century, Alfriston probably pre-dates the Mortlake *messuage* by a hundred years at least; but it is reasonable to suppose, even after allowing for some change in the late medieval vernacular architecture of south-east England, that they had much in common. Alfriston is a classic Wealden 'hall house' (depicted in the drawing below), and it seems a fair assumption that Dee's house would also have possessed a lofty central hall extending to the rafters, flanked on either side by ground and first floors, each with a single chamber. On this basis, the house would have had five rooms or more if there were partitions. Dee clearly made various additions, creating perhaps wings and annexes, but it is possible that some extensions were already in existence.

We can be a little more certain about the ground on which Dee's house once stood (see map on page 44). The 1617 survey confirms that this was between the High Street and the Thames, with the orchard and garden, as was often the case, on the other side of the road. There is also some indication, again from the survey, that the full extent of the property was about two to three acres.

This would seem to agree roughly with the modern 'footprint' of the site: the flats known as John Dee House, plus at least half the modern breadth of Mortlake High Street, and the riverside plot itself. Even a map as late as the 1913 Ordnance Survey shows how the property would have fitted into the old patterns of alleys and paths: the gap today between John Dee House and Craven House that was once Benhams Alley; Tapestry Alley with its water stairs; and, parallel to the High Street, Vineyard Path (or Bones Alley) that formed the south-facing boundary of Dee's orchard. There is also a match with the arable strips of the medieval Ewe Furlong, Dee's enclosed land being two strips wide and one third of a strip in length.[38]

Another important means of fixing Dee's property is Church Path. This runs diagonally from the Upper Richmond Road, across the Worple Way (and nowadays the railway), to the parish church. It is the old churchway, or corpseway, dating perhaps from 1543, the year the present church was built on the High Street.

The church tower of the new St. Marys, glimpsed from the fields, would surely have been an immediate landmark and would have attracted a short cut from the hamlet of East Sheen avoiding the longer way down Sheen Lane and the right-angle turn into the High Street. The path clearly respects the boundary wall of the Dee *messuage*, suggesting the latter's already well-established character.

It is possible that even in Dee's time this wall was of brick; and it is equally possible that the ancient wall that still stands between the Church and John Dee House contains contemporary Tudor brickwork (see photograph on page 50). An old gateway, thought to have been the back entrance to Dee's garden, or at least its immediate successor, certainly existed as recently as 1957, before the building of John Dee House.[39]

Dee himself also confirms the position of Church Path in relation to his garden wall. This is in his own famous account of the visit paid by Queen Elizabeth on 17 September 1580:

The Queen's Majesty came from Richmond in her coach, the higher way of Mortlake field. She turned down toward my house: and when she was against my garden in the field she stood there a good while, and then came into the street at the great gate of the field, where she espied me at my door making obeisance to her Majesty; she beckoned her hand for me; I came to her coach side, she very speedily pulled off her glove and gave me her hand to kiss: and to be short, asked me to resort to her court. [40]

From this it is clear that Elizabeth with her retinue, on catching sight of the Mortlake tower, made a detour along the churchway track between open fields. The Queen, it will be remembered, had followed the same route in 1575 when her visit coincided with the death of Dee's wife. But this time she was on horseback and it was the Earl of Leicester who helped her from the saddle 'by the Church wall of Mortlack'. When it was Dee's turn to engineer a meeting with the Queen, he likewise made use of the churchway. The first occasion, on 4 December, was when he was hoping to receive the sum of a hundred angels (gold coins) that the Queen had just promised him:

I met her at Eastshene gate, where she graciously, putting down her mask, did say with mery chere, I thank thee Dee; there was never promise made but it was broken or kept. [41]

Dee, typically, was to be disappointed of his hundred angels, as indeed he was on the second occasion. But what did the house accommodate? Taking again the Wealden 'hall house' as our putative point of departure, we have a house that grew in as many directions as possible; a house that was all angles, elevations and multiple levels. Given the nature of a site that would have precluded any forward encroachment on to Mortlake High Street, we can postulate some sideways development of the street facade if the width of the plot permitted it; but more likely would have been additions to the rear, perhaps extending even as far as the river bank and the public towpath. [42] It is also possible that Dee created annexes by incorporating existing outbuildings. Finally, there was always that London expedient, the loft conversion. Whether Dee ever built on the orchard and garden is not known, but one senses that he would not have subjected the plot to any 'grand design'. Perhaps what he created there was a simple 'philosopher's garden' for studious thought and recreation, a pleasance that was both a botanical resource and a living emblem of the harmony of creation.

Some of Dee's laboratories may have been housed in outbuildings or annexes – the noxiousness of fumes would have made that highly desirable. But we have Dee's own authority that the three laboratories leading off his main library were intended expressly for *Pyrotechnia* and other alchemical processes involving furnaces and flames. Goodwife Faldo, that repository of old Mortlake memories interviewed by Elias Ashmole in 1672, remembered that five or six stills were always bubbling away in the Dee house.

The centrepiece of the entire building, however, must surely have been the *Externa bibliotheca*, Dee's 'chief and open library'. For open it was: to visiting scholars and dignitaries, residential students and professional copyists, all desirous to consult its vast stock of manuscripts and printed books on a bewildering range of topics. Visitors, one supposes, would have been both welcome and unwelcome, their presence anything from a great honour to a great inconvenience. Dee, perhaps with a degree of irony, called his house *Mortlacensis Hospitali Philosophorum peregrinantium*: the Mortlake hospice (free hotel?) for wandering (errant?) philosophers. Francis Bacon visited, as did the voyager Richard Hakluyt, the governors of the Muscovy Company, and Sir Francis and Lady Walsingham, Dee's neighbours from Barn Elms.[43] Indeed everyone seemed to have acknowledged that the *Bibliotheca* was one of the great libraries of England, perhaps the greatest. Its sheer scale exceeded practically every other collection, and certainly those of the two universities and their constituent colleges. It would have been no exaggeration at the time to have claimed that the *Bibliotheca Mortlacensis* was among the most important in Europe.[44]

Title page of the 1620 edition of Christopher Marlowe's *Dr Faustus*

The obvious but by no means certain location of this great scientific academy would have to be the central hall of the house itself. Here, perhaps, was a room large enough and lofty enough to accommodate a large collection of books (as many perhaps as three or four thousand, including at least five hundred large folios) and well over a thousand manuscripts; it was also a room that would have been immediately accessible from the street. Against this theory, we have once again the colourful but not necessarily reliable voice of Goody Faldo, who insisted that Dee had '4 or 5 Roomes in his house fild with Bookes'. Perhaps this was overspill. Perhaps there really was an *Interna bibliotheca*. Who can say after four hundred years and a complete dearth of corroborating evidence? Perhaps the inner library was nothing more than Dee's own study and workbooks, or a series of schoolrooms.

Whatever the case, the tempting belief that there was a secret cache of demonic literature must be resisted. Dee may have been an occultist, but he was certainly no dabbler in 'cursed arts' and Faustian bargains.

The *Bibliotheca Mortlacensis* would no doubt have given off a rather business-like appearance, reflecting its utilitarian role as an intellectual resource or 'think tank'. This, after all, was no royal collection sumptuously appointed or lavishly housed, but a working library. Its atmosphere of studious chaos and clutter, dusty tomes and well-thumbed pages, was probably rather pleasant. Shelves, some horizontal and some vertical (as was the fashion) were everywhere, and ranged on them volumes with their spines showing and others (as was again the custom) with their edges pointing outwards. Some would have been bound *('libri compacti'),* others unbound *('libri non compacti'),* and Dee characteristically would not have been much bothered one way or the other. He certainly had no taste for fine bindings in his own house style and no manic tendency to classify and index[45]. Indeed his books appear to have been sorted chiefly according to size, while Dee himself was both catalogue and librarian. His memory, apparently, was prodigious and famous. When for example William Bourne, a successful writer on navigation, visited Mortlake and requested information regarding the number of ships under the command of the Emperor of China, Dee was able to locate a reference on the spot, and provide corroborative evidence from a second source.[46]

In addition to the Library and laboratories, further accommodation would have been needed for Dee's collection of 'rare and exquisitely made instruments mathematicall', his charters, seals and heraldic devices, all housed in what seems to have been a giant filing cabinet ('a great case or frame of boxes'), and last but not least his collection of natural wonders. The latter was doubtless the product of Dee's contacts with travellers and eminent explorers. It is not unreasonable to imagine a cabinet of curiosities that virtually took over an entire building: one that included plants, minerals, stuffed creatures, fossils, artefacts (archaeological and anthropological) and exotic costumes. Maps, according to the fashion of the day, might have been hung on the walls, with charts, globes and navigational instruments crowding every available surface.[47]

THE SIGILLUM DEI ÆMETH, A PANTACLE
MADE BY DR. JOHN DEE.
Figure V

Dee must have taken these collections very seriously. This is confirmed as early as 1568 in the *Propaedeumata Aphoristica*, the preface of which Dee signed *ex Musaeo nostro Mortlacensi*. The simple phrase 'from our Mortlake study' will not do, but the modern word 'museum' is also inaccurate. Perhaps we need to recall that in antiquity the great *mouseion* of Alexandria was in effect nothing short of a university. Dee's cabinet of curiosities therefore was no mere display case but a teaching resource on a grand scale. Dee may have exhibited obsessive curatorial instincts and jealousies, but there can be no denying his fundamental generosity and breadth of vision.

Dee, it seems, needed to keep open house and yet retreat into his own world of private study and angelic conversation. Here, the proximity of others was always a problem in a house of, at best, modest gentry proportions. In March 1582 the Archangel Michael, responding to concerns raised by Dee on that score, promised 'to shut the ears of them in the house, that none shall hear us'. A more practical remedy was to take over the most private room in the house, possibly one tucked away on its own upper floor under the eaves. If there really was an *Interna bibliotheca*, then such a chamber seems the most likely place. Perhaps the *Interna* was in fact Dee's own study or 'oratory'[48]. If so, an attic location in the part of the house symbolically most central and most elevated again seems obvious. Dee actually refers to such a room (the 'furthest little chamber' he calls it) in 1582, significantly just after Kelley's arrival, and insists that a bed first needs to be moved before it can be used. One imagines therefore an inner sanctum reached progressively room by room, floor by floor, in a way emblematic of Dee's own stages of initiation and enlightenment. Double doors,

54

when closed, would have been an absolute sign that nobody from the lower world was to enter: a single door would have permitted a cautious approach.

In the private study would have been the bibles and devotional writings lacking in the main library. There would also have been Dee's magical apparatus: the mirror, the gift of Sir William Pickering, that later would delight the Queen; a second mirror, of polished volcanic obsidian, dense and dark, that would eventually find its way to the British Museum; the show stone itself; and finally the books: Cornelius Agrippa's *De Occulta Philosophia*, the *Mystica Theologica* of Dionysius the Areopagite, the *Book of Soyga* with its spirit names and cabalistic codes, and Dee's collection of manuscripts by Ramon Lull, the Spanish mystical philosopher of the 13th century.

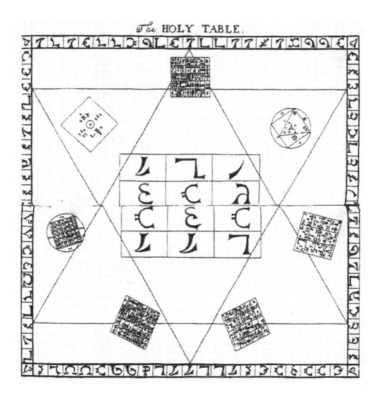

Also present, at the centre perhaps quite literally of Dee's world, would have been the 'Table of Practice' with its strange characters in the 'Enochian' alphabet and the crystal show stone itself. Chairs, a desk, a Turkish divan upholstered in green silk, and somewhere the famous cedar chest itself, would have furnished the room.[49] The chest was certainly talked about. A spirit visitor – 'El' – warned Dee specifically about it on 18 April 1583, saying that it had been discussed openly at Brentford. A further warning was issued: 'Your

55

chimney here will speak against you anon; yet I am no bricklayer.' Whereupon Dee confides in his diary: 'True it is, I had hidden there in a capcase the records of my doings with Saul and others etc.'

Books, certainly, were everywhere, especially in piles on the floor. On 28 May 1583, the angel Madimi in the form of a young girl made her first appearance to Dee and Kelley, picking her way delicately among the heaps:[50]

Suddenly there seemed to come out of my oratory a spiritual creature, like a pretty girl of seven or nine years of age, attired on her head with hair rolled up before and hanging down very long behind, with a gown of changeable green and red, and with a train.

She seemed to play up and down, child-like, and seemed to go in and out behind my books, lying on heaps: and as she should ever go between them, the books seemed to give place sufficiently, distinguishing one heap from the other, while she passed between them.

One cannot resist the suspicion that all this was pure theatre and that Kelley had coached a local child in the role.[51] The American historian Deborah Harkness has indeed argued convincingly that a great many of Kelley's 'visions' with their opening and closing curtains were dramatic in concept and employed both the language and spectacle of the stage.[52] Perhaps the world of 'theatre' was simply a convenient and powerful source of metaphor; but it is perfectly conceivable that Dee, in his enthusiasm, might have been induced to 'suspend his disbelief' during these carefully crafted performances. If such was the case, then the scene is one straight out of a Ben Jonson comedy – the 1610 play *The Alchemist* springs at once to mind – and John Dee is Edward's dupe or 'gull'.

It seems, too, that the oratory had a window facing Chiswick Reach. On 15 June 1583 at six o'clock on a summer evening Dee complained of too much light coming from the west window of his study and falling upon the table where the show stone was standing. Whereupon the angelic spirit Galvah sarcastically informed Dee that if he had too much light, she had too little, and what there was in any case came from the superior radiance of her own garments, and not from the sun. This abundance of light seems to confirm our earlier notion of an upper floor that was as close to the angels as possible and as far removed as was practical from the mundane distractions of a natural philosopher's *familia*.

So where in all this clutter were the domestic offices and private chambers? Pushed very much to one side, and very cramped, one imagines. In 1592, for instance, according to Dee's own reckoning in the *Compendious Rehearsall*, the household numbered seventeen: nine members of the immediate family and the

Dees' domestic servants, manservant and governess.[53] Wet nurses and gardeners would probably have been local people and therefore non-resident.[54] But others – laboratory assistants, the in-house 'scryrer', the master's pupils and his occasional visitors – would have swelled the number.[55] Indeed during the last months of 1592, the Dees accommodated no less than an entire family: that of Anthony Ashley whose wife had just survived serious illness.[56] Such considerations suggest, without exaggeration, a round figure of some twenty people residing in the Mortlake house at any one time. Even allowing for the 16th century's very different standards of privacy, the Dee household was as crowded as it was remarkable.

It is this, and the master and mistress of this unusual household, that we must now consider.

---

[34] Mortlake was in the manor of Wimbledon, hence the location of the manorial court. The church would have been St Mary's, yet another dedication to the Blessed Virgin in this area.

[35] The 1617 survey is kept by the Northamptonshire County Record Office.

[36] See Leslie Freeman *Going to the Parish* (1993).

[37] This interesting drawing was once in the collection of the antiquary William Upcott (1779-1845) but its earlier provenance in unfortunately unknown.

[38] The strips of the Ewe Furlong ran from the river as far inland as the Worple Way (ie the modern railway track).

[39] See the photograph on page 21 of *Alleyways of Mortlake and East Sheen* by Charles Hailstone (1983) – on page 27 of the 2009 edition. See also the entries on Bones Alley, Church Path and Vineyard Path.

[40] The Queen had clearly reached Mortlake High Street from the modern Upper Richmond Road by means of the main gate intended to prevent cattle straying on to the open fields via the churchway. Dee's front door would probably have opened directly on to the High Street.

[41] Not to be confused with Richmond Park. This was clearly the gate at the Sheen end of the churchway, corresponding to the 'great gate' at the Mortlake end.

[42] All later buildings in this immediate area abutted directly onto the river.

[43] Bacon, perhaps inspired by Mortlake, advocated in 1594 the establishment of a centre of scholarship with a library, a garden, a cabinet of natural and artificial phenomena, and finally a still-house.

[44] For a more detailed discussion of the Library see Chapter 4, *Bibliotheca Mortlacensis*.

[45] Unlike Samuel Pepys almost a hundred years later. The *Bibliotheca Pepysiana* is now housed at Magdalene College, Cambridge.

[46] Recorded in Bourne's own *Regiment for the Sea* (1580). Quoted by William Sherman in *John Dee, the Politics of Reading*.

[47] We know that Dee had at least two globes produced by the great Flemish cartographer Gerardus Mercator.

[48] References abound in the Dee diaries. Perhaps 'study' and 'oratory' are the one and the same place, although Dee does make a distinction between praying at the table in his study and praying in his oratory. It is possible that the latter was a small annexe.

[49] See the Epilogue.

[50] Dee was to name his second daughter Madimia, born in February 1590 in Mortlake.

[51] Or his stepdaughter, Elizabeth Jane Weston, later 'Westonia' the poetess (see note 65). The only problem here is that she might have been too young in the year 1583 to play such a part.

[52] Deborah Harkness, *Shows in the Showstone: A Theater of Alchemy and Apocalypse in the Angel Conversations of John Dee*.

[53] John and Jane Dee and seven children make nine. The eighth child, Margaret, was yet to be born, in August 1595.

[54] The wet nurses, certainly, were local. The reference on 4 August 1581 to Katherine, Dee's eldest daughter, is typical: 'Katharn was sent home from Nurse Maspely of Barnes for fear of her man's sickness: and Goodwife Benet gave her suck'. Katherine, born at 7.30am on June 7, would have been two months old.

[55] One laboratory assistant was the alchemist Roger Cook, who cantankerously served Dee for fifteen awkward years.

[56] Ashley was Clerk to the Privy Council and author of *The Mariner's Mirror of Navigation* (1588).

Chapter 3

A Mortlake Ménage

A visitor one morning to the home of Dr John Dee in the riverside village of Mortlake during the early 1580s might first have encountered Walter Hooper, the Chiswick gardener, giving Dr Dee's hedges and knots their twice yearly trimming (for the price of five shillings, meat and drink included). If not he, then perhaps the melancholy Roger Cook will be in evidence, toiling away somewhere in the laboratories. This is a notoriously difficult man, and his grumblings will almost certainly be recorded in the Dee diary at the end of the day (but always discreetly, in the Greek letters known only to the master). George, the manservant, will probably be up a ladder, or falling off one; and if it

A present day photograph showing the Watergate Steps

is 3 July 1582, just after midday, Arthur Dee, the eldest child, will this minute have fallen from the top of the Watergate Stairs (stairs that still exist now - four hundred years later) and have cut open his forehead above the right eyebrow. A few years later, Mary Goodwyn, governess to the Dee daughters, will be present; or else Mr Lee, the Mortlake schoolmaster, come to receive his stipend. The master himself is probably closeted in his study; but it is almost certain that the mistress, Jane Fromond Dee, will be very visible, managing and supervising the household of England's greatest natural philosopher.

Marriage to Dr John Dee would have been no easy matter. Yet without the Reformation it would never have occurred, and Jane Fromond's spouse-to-be would have been a celibate clerk in holy orders. A hundred or so years later this same scientific household will have disappeared, because natural philosophy will now be housed independently of the home. Mistress Dee's establishment, for all its individual quirkiness, is therefore wholly characteristic of the early modern period and the transitional nature of the knowledge economy.

The self-sufficient household of the Middle Ages was already disappearing, giving way to a family unit grounded on wage-earning and shopping, supported in towns and cities by the growth of the professional and mercantile classes. A wife such as Jane Dee would now have found herself in a less productive role, encouraged instead to embellish and manage her husband's home and reflect his local status; while Dee, as a professional man, would steadily have colonised his wife's traditional domestic space. Such co-existence would have created a problematic and sometimes volatile situation for the couple, for all their commitment to the traditional principle of marriage as partnership. Certainly, on a purely practical level, Dee's activities would have interfered with Jane's and it is perfectly possible that his local reputation for wizardry would have compromised her reputation as a virtuous 'helpmeet'.

We know very little of Jane's origins, other than that she was born in 1555, the daughter of Bartholomew Fromond of East Cheam in Surrey and was connected in some way to the entourage of Lady Clinton, a lady-in-waiting to the Queen.[57] This suggests gentry origins, and perhaps also how she came to marry Dee, who had connections of his own at court. Socially, she would have been an equal if not a decidedly superior partner. Brought up from an early age with the help of conduct books and much practical experience to manage a substantial household, Jane Fromond would have graced her marriage with many domestic accomplishments. Her responsibilities would have included supervision of all cooking activities, preparation of simple remedies and cosmetics, the management of servants and wagging tongues, the care of clothing and linen, her own children's welfare, and her husband's thrift and hospitality. The latter would have presented particular difficulties; for although the Dees kept, in the words of Goody Faldo, a 'plentifull table' befitting their gentry status, there was never sufficient money for both that and the expense of a parallel scientific establishment. The latter required wealthy and even royal patrons, and to attract and entertain them required first of all a very ample outlay. Jane Dee was caught here in a double bind: on the one hand she had to maintain the appearance of a prosperous, genteel and hospitable household; on the other she had to eke out her family's limited assets.

She seems to have had more than her fair share of domestic problems. Two maids, Jane Gaele and Mary Cunstable, set fire to their room twice in a single year, and Nurse Ann Frank, 'tempted by a wicked spirit', ran amok, despite her own master's application of holy oil, and threw herself down a well before expiring in her own room upstairs. George, Dee's personal servant, disgraced himself in a bout of binge-drinking one December night in 1582 and returned home in the morning to heap verbal abuse on the family. He was finally dismissed on 7 July 1583. The laboratory assistants would have been even more difficult to contain. Dee, it seems, deliberately sought out 'melancholics' (we might call them manic depressives) for their susceptibility to divine and astral influence. For Jane, however, these men would have been anti-social and moody irritants, a situation aggravated by their being educated well beyond ordinary domestic servants and, it has to be said, most women. Roger Cook for example was always creating occasions to leave the Dee's employ. Edward Kelley had certainly been accused of counterfeiting and had used at least one alias; while he, Richard Walkdyne and Robert Web were all at one time or another taken into custody by the Mortlake magistrates.

Awkwardly placed and unable, because her husband was unwilling, to draw a clear line with these men, Jane Dee was often under considerable stress. It is hardly surprising that she took an immediate dislike to Edward Kelley the moment he appeared as 'Mr Talbot' in March 1582, and went on to resent the way he monopolized her husband's time, resources and enthusiasm. On 6 May, just two months after his arrival, Jane cracked, provoked by Kelley's sudden and exasperating allegation that her husband and Mr Clerkson, (the agent who sometimes introduced scryers) had been duped by Barnabas Saul. Enough was enough. A line had to be drawn. It is also possible that Dee, in his eagerness to accommodate the Archangel Michael, had just mentioned to her the bed that required moving from the upper room. Whatever he said, he was clearly shaken by the violence of her reaction. This was in due course recorded:

> *Jane, in a marvellous rage at 8 of the clock at night till 11½ and all that night and next morning till 8 of the clock, melancholic and choleric terribly for the cozening . . . some used that come to me as honest and learned men . . . by Mr Clerkson his brother was directed.*

Some time later these distraught and incoherent fragments would be crossed out by a contrite husband.

Yet Dee's pursuit of angelic conversations continued. Scientific observation of the physical world and long hours of study were in themselves not enough by the 1580s for John Dee. His firm belief that contact with spirits alone would lead to 'true wisdome' was now unshakeable, as was his belief in the special gifts of the men he used. He was, he knew, no visionary himself; but he could at least make himself a worthy participant by leading an exemplary and pure life. Jane must have felt very cut off sometimes, and even resentful, with the routines of her household so upset and its finances so compromised.[58] And sooner or later it would have become blindingly obvious that the 'angels' did not pay bills and that the alternative, 'astrology by appointment', was far more lucrative. She would also have had to worry about prying eyes, awkward visitors and unpreventable local gossip.

The situation brought on by Kelley's influence continued for a long while, not only during Kelley's relatively brief Mortlake period between March 1582 and September 1583 (when, as we have seen, Kelley introduced the added complication of a wife) but also during the entire household's removal to Poland and Bohemia. Yet Kelley's continued presence, however irksome his tantrums and his parasitical use of the house must have been, had to be borne because he was needed. Here, Jane would have had two alternatives: to scream or to be silent. The conduct books of her youth would have counselled the latter; her forthright character the former. Dee, for his part, was always relieved when Jane was in a better mood and on better terms with Kelley. Such was the case on 26 April 1583 when Kelley returned to the house after a disagreement, his 'vehement passions and pangs' for once pacified, and Dee gratefully noted that Jane was 'very willing' to welcome him back to her household and was herself now 'quieted in mind, and very friendly'. This perhaps says a great deal for Jane's magnanimity and her loyalty to her husband's interests.

There is also some evidence that Jane herself was sympathetic towards angelic conversations and even a firm believer in them. Yet it might have been sheer desperation ('perplexity' is Dee's word in the diary) that drove her in March 1585 to consult the angels about the dire financial straits of her expatriate household in Prague. In a direct written petition, but submitted of course through her husband and Kelley, she drew the spirits' attention to the 'necessity' they were all in. She also made it clear that it was unbecoming to the godliness of her husband's 'Actions' that he was having to resort to pawning 'the ornaments of our house, and the coverings of our bodies' among the Jews and other ill-disposed citizens of the city.[59] The reply she received – whether it came from Kelley, her husband, or a perfectly orthodox chauvinistic angel of the 16th century – was wholly predictable: she, a mere woman, had been too presumptuous in coming to the 'synagogue' with her petition. There would indeed be 'one storm' to come (a domestic disagreement?),which she would have to take quietly for her own good ('thou shalt be the more whiter'); but she and her children would not be abandoned by God. With this reassurance, she was then commanded to remember that she was 'yoked' to her marriage and required to be 'faithful and obedient'. The best thing for everyone would be for her to stop her 'murmuring' and make amends by sweeping her house.

Jane's reaction is unfortunately not recorded, but the incident, as recorded by Dee, certainly suggests that she had been put firmly in her place. Perhaps Dee was tacitly recognizing his wife's household trials and tribulations, but he was also confirming that she was not to call into question either his authority or his professional activities. The Judaeo-Christian allusion to his private study as 'the synagogue' makes it plain that natural philosophy had patriarchal status and would always prevail. So it was that an issue begun one March day in Mortlake was settled at a place a thousand miles to the east and two years later in time. Perhaps this was the *fait accompli* that returned with John and Jane Dee to Mortlake after their European travels and remained in place for the rest of their married life.

Yet one senses, even across the great gap of more than four hundred years, that not all Jane's difficulties were caused by her husband and his profession. There is also something highly strung about Jane herself, and it is just possible that she suffered from some form of mild mental illness. To suggest manic depression is to take things much too far; but given the number of pregnancies she underwent (eight in all, plus at least two miscarriages, in 1580 and 1593) one can tentatively suggest a state of almost continuous post-natal depression over a twenty-year period. There is also some evidence, from her husband's records of her menstruation, that she was prone to erratic and even missed periods, although to be quite sure of this we have also to be certain – which we can never be – that Dee recorded each and every one as a matter of paramount importance.

Jane certainly displayed violent mood swings and irascibility, and one of the most disturbing instances of her temper was the occasion in 1589 at Bremen, on the family's homeward journey from Bohemia, when she gave her six-year-old daughter Katherine such a heavy blow on the ear that it caused considerable bruising and seriously ruptured a blood vessel in the nose. It is likely that such violence was well beyond the level of parental chastisement considered acceptable even by the standards of the 16th century: on the other hand the blow might simply have been unfortunate. Dee's diary certainly seems to record something shocking and out of the ordinary, but it is significant that no judgement was passed.

Jane's illnesses are well-recorded. During the night of 15 July 1582 she was troubled with 'a colic cramp in her belly' and in the morning vomited green bile, but was sufficiently recovered later in the day to take to the water and travel to Petersham to pay Nurse Garrett her twelve shillings wages. This perhaps suggests that the problem was nothing more than a passing abdominal upset. More worrying, though, was an illness in Prague, in 1584. Dee himself was concerned, and from the diary entry – 'the state of my wife her grievous disease' – we form the impression that it had been around for some while. What is of particular interest is that Dee links Jane's problem to her emotional state and hopes that she will be 'of a quieter mind, and not so testy and fretting as she is'. When the angels were consulted, Gabriel's answer was unequivocal: Jane and the child she was carrying were in a dangerous and even life-threatening situation. The next day Dee pressed Gabriel for more information.

The ensuing angelic diagnosis of Jane Dee is at once complex and vague, and not easy for a non-specialist reader of today to understand. It is therefore reassuring to know that it was probably never anything more than Kelley's own shot at a neo-Paracelsian[60] medical opinion. Even in the 17th century it was dismissed as 'rare stuff, most part of it, for a quack'.[61] The gist seems to be that an imperfection in her mother's womb had developed after Jane's conception, probably owing to a fever, and that the delicacy it caused went unnoticed in her childhood 'by reason of the spiritual heat in youth'. At the age of sixteen, when Jane began menstruating, the effects began to manifest themselves more openly, and in her latest pregnancy (she being 'foetive') they had become very serious indeed. The 'force of heat' was now being drawn to the nutriment of the 'creature' (the child) causing great weakness in the mother and making her unable to carry out 'excremental expulsion'. What again is interesting is that there follows yet another reference to Jane's mental state. This time it is suggested that her health is being impeded by 'imagination', by her dark and pessimistic thoughts. Of course Kelley may have been behind this, as it would surely have been in his interest to make Jane appear more emotional and hysterical than she really was – but the fact remains that her pregnancy with Michael, a sickly child who died young, was a difficult one.[62] Perhaps the whole thing was psychosomatic. Perhaps Jane Dee's underlying instability, if we assume that it was her problem, manifested itself only at especially stressful moments of domestic crisis and pregnancy. If so, we have rather to admire her courage and self-control, and also her willingness to undergo the regular ordeals of 16th century childbirth, especially if she was battling against hysteria and depression. Above all she was a conscientious, loyal and hardworking wife, and when Dee called her his 'paineful Jane' he surely meant it in every sense of the word. His later concern, this time for the ulcer on her right ankle that finally burst on 18 February 1597 after five days of excruciating pain, is also unmistakable, though not at first obvious.[63]

By modern standards Dee's terse records of his wife's wellbeing may strike us as stoical and even unfeeling. But the diary, it must be realised, is first and foremost an early scientific and practical document, not a romantic journal tracking a myriad of personal impressions and soulful sensibilities. Dee does not even record the treatment Jane received for the ulcer, let alone whether it healed properly; but he does faithfully record the 'remedy' proposed by Gabriel for Jane's earlier disease during pregnancy: pure wheat, one live cock pheasant, eleven ounces of white amber, and an ounce and a quart of turpentine. Dee objected that he would not be able to find a pheasant (this is Bohemia, he says – but Gabriel gives him short shrift); and then we hear no more. Whether this concoction, pounded in red wine and then boiled, was ever given to Jane we shall never know, let alone whether it did her any good. Perhaps Dee lost interest once the essential ingredient of the cock pheasant proved so elusive. Such is the Dee diary.

The fertility of the Dee marriage, though not remarkable by Elizabethan standards, adds a further dimension to the Mortlake ménage. Here again, Jane's role as a woman was made problematic by her husband's practice of natural philosophy. Wives in the 16th century were required above all to be chaste – faithful, that is, to their husbands and ready to be fruitful despite the pains of childbirth. Chastity, therefore, was family planning, not celibacy or abstinence, although of course the lusts of the flesh were always to be avoided. Dee, as a natural philosopher in the tradition of Cornelius Agrippa, would have been particularly mindful of this. Perfect marital chastity, for the accomplishment of his great scientific purpose, would have been every bit as important as spiritual purity. Dee's record keeping of both Jane's menstrual cycles and the dates and times of their love-making was clearly very important, and evidence, in the words of Deborah Harkness, that he took charge of his wife's fruitfulness by 'scrutinizing and orchestrating their sexual relations'. [64] He was, in effect, keeping a regular account of the chastity of his marriage. At the same time one cannot help feeling that such interest was aroused as much by the astrological implications of childbirth. Perhaps Dee was investigating whether it was better to calculate 'nativities' from the date of birth or from the moment of conception. The astrological annotations and planetary positions that accompany some of Dee's family records seem to suggest such an interest. What is inescapable is that natural philosophy, having invaded Jane's domestic space, went on to appropriate her body as yet another laboratory. It can be argued that the menstrual cycles and sexual activity of Jane Dee make her one of the most intimately known and still unknown women of the early modern period.

Jane Dee was also a participant in one of the most bizarre domestic arrangements of the Elizabethan period, one that would not have sat at all easily with the couple's shared notions of chastity. This is of course the notorious case of 'cross-matching' between the Dees and the Kelleys that occurred between April and May 1587 at Třeboň in Bohemia, at a time when Dee's endeavours in Europe were wholly dominated by angelic conversation, alchemy and Kelley. His relationship with this volatile man – never an easy one – was now under even greater strain. Kelley was freelancing and beginning to make a name for himself as an alchemist at the court of Rudolf II, and Dee, meanwhile, was more and more dependent on him to further the urgent work of understanding God's creation. In fact, the urgency was such that Dee was beginning to make use of his eldest son Arthur, now aged almost eight, as a stand-in. The angels, seeing this, offered to repair the rift between the two men: Dee and Kelley, they said, would from now on hold all things in common: their alchemical secrets, the angelic revelations – and their wives.

The lurking figure of Edward Kelley is unmistakable in all this. Perhaps he was testing the kind of hold he still had on Dee, especially if he was resentful of the upstart Arthur Dee. On the other hand, his seeming reluctance to carry out the angels' bidding might have been genuine; which suggests that, with prospects now of his own, he had simply invented the 'cross-matching' as a way of drawing his actions with Dee to a close. If this is so, then there is a strong possibility that he never expected Dee to agree to such an arrangement. More convincing perhaps is the simple theory that he wanted to father the child that his wife had not been able to give him.[65] There is even the possibility that he had long concealed a sexual interest in Jane Dee.

It is highly significant therefore that the first reference to Joanna Kelley's barrenness occurs only a month before. This was on 4 April 1587, when the spirit spoke directly to Kelley:

> *As unto thee, barrenness dwelleth with thee because thou didst neglect me, and take a wife unto thyself contrary to my commandment.*[66]

Things now began to move swiftly: God would soon bless them with greater insights into the workings of Nature.

John Dee was horrified of course, but was also sufficiently credulous, or so totally dedicated to his work, to take the matter seriously. Over dinner on the evening of 18 April he spoke openly for the first time to the two wives:

> *After our going out of the chapel, and our being at dinner . . . I found means to make some little declaration of our great grief (mine chiefly) now occasioned, either to try us, or really to be executed, in the common and indifferent way of matrimonial acts amongst any couple of us four:*

which thing was strange to the women: and they hoped of some more comfortable issue of the cause. And so we left off.

Later that night at 2 am, after further prompting from the spirits, Dee finally made his way to bed, where he found Jane still awake:

I then told her, and said: 'Jane, I see there is no other remedy, but as hath been said of our cross-matching, so it needs must be done.'

Thereupon she fell a-weeping and trembling for a quarter of an hour, and I pacified her as well as I could: and so, in the fear of God, and in believing of his admonishment, did persuade her, that she showed herself prettily resolved to be content for God his sake and his secret purposes, to obey the admonishment.

At length that same night in bed she yielded to do the commanded doctrine, and requested that we might all have our lodgings in one chamber, that I might not be far from her.

'I trust,' said she, 'though I give myself thus to be used, that God will turn me into stone before he would suffer me, in my obedience, to receive any shame or inconvenience.'

In the middle of the next night, 19-20 April, John Dee and Jane Dee made love. The same occurred at two o'clock on the afternoon of 24 April. The following day Jane menstruated.

Meanwhile Dee was once more doubting the truth and integrity of Edward Kelley. But the admonition of God through the angels became stronger than ever:

'Your wife is dear to you, your wisdom dearer, and I myself am the dearest of all. Having been chosen you tremble, and by hesitating you sin. All these things are from me, and permissible to you. I admonish you as the children of God, to consider your vocation . . .'

On 3 May the pact between the two couples was drawn up on paper and duly signed. On 6 May all four, but chiefly the women, felt that final approval of the pact should be sought from God. The puckish girl-spirit Madimi appeared and at once confirmed everything:

'It is decided. Make haste. Let everything be in common among you.'

67

Yet haste was there none. It was now Kelley's turn to prevaricate. He cut the pact in two and gave the Dees the half with their signatures, retaining the other. And there matters stood. Whether Kelley was enjoying the delay and the advantage it gave him or was beginning to experience genuine moral scruples, we shall never know. Perhaps he was even waiting for the moment when Jane Dee would be at her most fertile. There is certainly evidence that he read Dee's diaries.

The next significant development occurred on 20 May, when Madimi again appeared and, using her finger, made the two pieces of paper whole again. Then a voice was heard:

> *'He that pawneth his soul for me loseth it not, and he that dieth for me, dieth to eternal life. For I will lead you in the way of knowledge and understanding: and judgement and wisdom shall be upon you, and shall be restored unto you: and you shall grow every day wise and mighty in me.'*

This was later read by Dee to the two wives; whereupon Kelley told Joanna that God had confirmed in his mind 'all good purposes' and that he was now resolved not to ride out on other business but to remain in the house instead. This seems to have set the seal. The following day, 21 May, at an hour unknown, Dee recorded tersely in his diary: *Pactum factum.* In other words, the agreement had been put into practice. Beyond this, Dee's diary is silent. Part of the relevant page has been cut with a knife or scissors, and what further record or observation there might have been has been lost for ever. We do not even know if the 'cross-matching' was repeated.[67] As Deborah Harkness remarks, this was the most severe blow that natural philosophy ever dealt Jane Dee, the virtuous and painstaking Elizabethan housewife. The issues that it raised went far beyond her domestic management and her husband's separate prerogatives.

There was at least one consequence of the 'cross-matching': the child Theodore Dee, conceived during this bizarre episode and born on 28 February 1588, two days after an eclipse, with Mercury in the ascendant, and nine months to the day after the consummation. The likelihood therefore that Kelley was his father is strong, perhaps compelling. Dee certainly records that his wife ceased menstruating in June, so there can be little chance that Theodore was premature. The next record, of Jane's bleeding four months into her pregnancy, suggests Dee's very real fear of a miscarriage, and perhaps argues that he attached special significance to this fifth pregnancy. More illuminating than anything else, however, is the child's name at the christening on 1 March 1588: *Theodorus Trebonianus Dee* – 'God's gift at Třeboň'.

68

Theodore left his native Bohemia and returned with the family to Mortlake towards the end of 1589, an arduous journey for an infant still in his second year. Thereafter, the life of Theodore Dee, as recorded in the diary, is absorbed into the day-to-day concerns of his father and the childhood ailments and accidents of his siblings. His 'tertian ague' and bloodshot eye take their places with Arthur's 'quotidian ague' and knocking himself out with a brick, with Roland's falling into the Thames and Madimia's falling out of bed. Yet one still senses that Dee had a special feeling for the child of his last great 'Action' with Edward Kelley.

The doctrine of 'cross-matching', however, came to nothing. The death of Theodore in Manchester in 1601, aged thirteen, must have seemed to Dee like a judgement, and it is a great pity that we have no record of anyone's feelings at this very sad time.[68] Dee himself would now have been seventy-three years of age. Perhaps he came finally to accept that the greater part of his life's work was at an end and that God had reclaimed as much as He had ever bestowed. And what Jane might have felt is even more difficult to infer. Perhaps Theodore was no more to her than her other children. Perhaps he was a disturbing reminder of Kelley. We shall never know.

Unfortunately Jane herself left no surviving record of her experiences. There is, however, just one letter remaining in her own bold hand, written from Třeboň early in 1587. It is addressed to her husband, who had that very morning left for Prague:

> *Sweetheart. I commend me unto you, hoping in God that you are in good health as I, and my children, with all my household, am here, I prayse God for it. I have none other matter to write unto you at this time.*

These are the direct, affectionate and distinctly educated words of an Elizabethan gentlewoman a thousand miles from her native land. There is, as Charlotte Fell Smith observed, a capable and managing sound to 'my children' and 'my household'. Written at the age of thirty-two, after nine years of marriage to John Dee, the letter seems to express acceptance of how things were. Jane perhaps came to believe in her husband's angels or at least tactfully to put up with them. The return to Mortlake after the years of peregrination in Europe must have been a relief, no matter how much the Mortlake house had been disturbed in her absence: but the removal to Manchester in February 1596, after just six years of relative stability in her original marital home, must again have demanded all her courage, resilience, energy and loyalty.[69] Her death in that city from plague in 1605, together with two if not three of her children, brought the household she had run 'painfully' for her husband for over twenty-five years to a formal close. Hers is a sad story.

[57] Dee himself always used the form 'Fromonds'.

[58] A typical example of domestic interruption, from 1582, occurred when Dee suggested breaking off an Action 'by reason of the folk tarrying for supper', only to be told by the Archangel Michael 'lay down the world, and continue your work'.

[59] In *A Compendious Rehearsall* Dee admits that he once pawned his wife's jewellery but does not say when and where.

[60] Paracelsus – Philippus Theofrastus von Hohenheim (1493-1541) was a German-Swiss physician whose influence was considerable in Dee's lifetime. His medical practice relied strongly on astrology, but he also taught that sickness and health were dependent on man's harmony with natural order and that effective treatments could be found in herbs and minerals.

[61] *A True and Faithful Relation of what passed for many years between Dr John Dee and Some Spirits*, Meric Casaubon (London, 1659).

[62] Michael, born 22 February 1585, died aged nine on 13 July 1594.

[63] The ulcer on the right lower *talus* was said to be 'in the accustomed place' – a disturbing detail.

[64] Deborah Harkness, *Managing an Experimental Household: The Dees of Mortlake and the Practice of Natural Philosophy*.

[65] Another theory, preferred by Dilys Henrik Jones, is that Joanna Kelley was the widow of Francis Weston and had borne him two children, Elizabeth Jane Weston and John Francis Weston. Elizabeth was later famous in Prague as the neo-Latin poet 'Westonia'. It is, of course, possible that Joanna Kelley became infertile after the birth of Elizabeth and her brother.

[66] Is this the conscience of a lapsed Catholic priest speaking?

[67] The diary entry for 23 May 1587 gives the impression that the 'act of obedience' had been found sufficient and 'accepted'.

[68] The diary breaks off just days before this sad event. Was Dee perhaps too broken or too numb to continue with it?

[69] Diary entries during the later Mortlake period include a reference to Jane's 'impatience' on 21 July 1591 – a time when she would have been three months pregnant with her final child, Frances. There were also at least two outbursts of anger, one of them definitely provoked by her maids.

The catalogue of Dee's Library showing *Taken* and *Fromond*

71

Chapter 4

The Bibliotheca Mortlacensis

Any account of the *Bibliotheca Mortlacensis* of John Dee, however superficial, must pay immediate tribute to the work of Julian Roberts and Andrew Watson, whose facsimile edition with commentary of the 1583 Library catalogue is an outstanding example of bibliographical scholarship.[70] As outstanding, only this time as an academic history of ideas and a discussion of the practice of reading in the early modern period, is William Sherman's book on the function of the Dee library in 16th century England. This American scholar, through a masterly study of Dee's annotations and marginalia, offers us a convincing insight into the way Dee read his books and made use of them. Both the Library catalogue and Sherman have done Dee a great service. Now, after more than four hundred years, Dee is again the 'intelligencer' that his educated and often distinguished contemporaries recognised, and not the 'magus', or worse, of idle gossip and legend.

The *Bibliotheca*, as we have seen, was a house of knowledge, a resource by the standards of Elizabethan England on a vast scale and a central feature of Dee's Mortlake property. In 1592, some years after the wholesale pilfering of books that occurred during his continental absence, Dee could speak wistfully of his 'late library room', either because it was no more or because he was being denied access to it by Nicholas Fromond.[71]

It was in fact the European journey (1583-89) that led Dee in the first place to catalogue his library. The resulting document, with its 2292 books and 198 manuscripts, is dated 6 September 1583, about a fortnight before the household left Mortlake. Dee took about 800 books from the library. These books are clearly marked 'T' (= taken). The others, marked 'F', are the ones left in the care of Fromond. Dee's choice of books clearly reflected the purpose of his journey: two-thirds of his collection on alchemy and almost ninety percent of the bound Paracelsian, hermetic and cabalist stock went with him. It should be appreciated that these figures correspond to individual titles, not to the multiple copies that were left behind. Dee had a great many of these in certain subjects, which argues that his Library was indeed used for public reference and for teaching. Dee also took with him a number of scientific and mathematical works, but there is little evidence from the spirit diaries that he made much use of them. Neither is there much evidence of book-buying in Europe on this occasion.

The first 1400 entries in the catalogue are in effect a shelf-catalogue, reflecting the fact, noted already in Chapter 2, that Dee's arrangement of books was largely according to size. This system, however, eventually breaks off and other patterns begin to emerge: specialist areas such as alchemy, Paracelsian magic, navigation, Hebrew, and also clutches of early editions suggesting bulk purchase from the estates of deceased collectors. There were also the multiple copies: Dee for example possessed 92 editions of Paracelsus in 157 copies. The catalogue certainly appears to have been very thorough, even exhaustive: yet there survive 22 books with an undisputed Dee provenance that do not appear in it.

The largest books – the folios – were about five hundred in number. About three-quarters were bound (*compacti*): inevitably, only a few of the unbound or disbound copies have survived. Dee was usually careful to write his name in his books, often Latinised as *Joannes Deëus* and sometimes transcribed in Greek. This seems to suggest both pride of ownership and a precaution against 'borrowing'. However, even when a signature is missing, there are annotations – sometimes extensive – in Dee's unmistakable hand. It is perhaps surprising that no armorial bookplates have been found, given Dee's interest in family pedigrees and his armigerous instincts.

Also surprising are the gaps in Dee's otherwise extraordinarily compendious library. There is for example very little theology.[72] Following contemporary practice, the first two books in the catalogue are Biblical Concordances, but then the customary sequence breaks off.[73] Law, too, is conspicuously absent. Also thin on the ground, surprisingly, are Dee's own works. But Paracelsus, Aristotle, Euclid, Ptolemy and Agrippa, in that order, are the Library's great strengths. Of particular interest is the comprehensive collection of contemporary and essentially ephemeral pamphlets on astronomical events: the comets of 1577 and 1580, and, most spectacular of all, the 'portentous' nova of 1572. Dee also possessed significant amounts of Arab astronomy, translated into Latin, which suggest a strong early attraction to that subject. There is on the other hand little evidence that alchemy was of much appeal to the younger Dee, although an interest in mining and metallurgy might have led in that direction. Medical, herbal and botanical works, as one would expect in a natural philosopher's library, are well represented.

Less expected, perhaps, are Dee's books on the arts and architecture. It is significant that of the thirty-nine treatises published in England between 1560 and 1620, Dee owned no fewer than fourteen by 1583. He had also by this date collected most of the Greek and Roman classical authors then available in print. Yet there is no edition of the complete works of Sophocles in the original Greek – a surprising omission for the former Under-reader of Trinity College. Sophocles, however, is at least covered in Latin translation and in various pocket selections in the original language. There is also a marked neglect of English literature, the only work by Chaucer being *The Treatise on the Astrolabe*, while Shakespeare, an obscure upstart from the West Midlands, is completely absent. But works in German, French, Italian, Flemish, Spanish and Welsh do feature, suggesting, along with Dee's well-attested Latin, Greek and Hebrew, the identity of a polyglot scholar with a working knowledge of no fewer than nine foreign languages. It is also possible that Dee acquired more than a smattering of Polish and Czech, which would have brought the total to no less than eleven.

On the other hand, and for all Dee's antiquarianism, there is no Anglo-Saxon material of any kind, not even the monumental 1571 edition of the Gospels. But it seems that he at least read widely in British history. He possessed three valuable manuscripts of Geoffrey of Monmouth's *Historia Regnum Britanniae* as well as the great printed edition of 1517. The existence of the manuscripts argues strongly that he must have played some part in rescuing important material from the monastic libraries. His early advocacy of a national library during the reign of Mary may have come to nothing, but his creation of the *Bibliotheca* at least kept alive the principle of a national collection. It is satisfying to know, but also ironic, that some of Dee's books and manuscripts have found their way finally to the British Library. As a bibliophile and antiquarian Dee was, as in all things, a loyal subject (the word 'patriotic' is probably too modern for an Elizabethan); but the evidence of the Library suggests that he was also very proud of his Welsh ancestry. Whenever an early book surfaces with the name of King Arthur emphatically underlined in a contemporary hand, there is always a good chance of a John Dee provenance.

This, roughly, was the Library entrusted to Nicholas Fromond. It is almost impossible to know for certain what kind of relationship Dee had with his brother-in-law. The diaries seem to suggest that it was rather distant, based purely on ties of formal kinship. It may even be that Nicholas Fromond felt that his sister had not always been well used and was therefore inclined to fight her corner. Fromond certainly did not take at all kindly to being left to pay his brother-in-law's book bill of £63 13s 8¼d presented by Andreas Freemonsheim, the London-based agent of the Cologne firm of Birkmann. He obstinately refused to settle it, and relations between the brothers-in-law were not on a regular footing again until April 1592.

With books such a sensitive issue it was perhaps unfortunate that the possibly philistine Fromond appeared to take so little care of the great library. Tradition has it that he negligently allowed it to be ransacked by a Mortlake mob out either for gain or to make some point about its absent owner.[74] Those with strong local feelings will therefore be pleased to know that Roberts and Watson have exonerated the 'Mortlake mob' by denying its very existence. The finger of suspicion, indeed of accusation, points elsewhere.

Firstly to the seaman John Davis (c.1552-1605). The incriminating annotation 'John Davis spoyle' in Dee's own hand occurs some seventy times, and in one instance the dark phrase 'by violence' is added. Davis is thought to have had an interest in the spirit world and in scrying generally, but he was really a veteran of three unsuccessful attempts at finding the Northwest Passage. He is also credited with the discovery that Greenland is not part of the North American continent. Roberts and Watson believe that Davis had become so exasperated by Dee's loss of interest in the Passage that he simply broke into the Library. That he helped himself more in haste and in anger is evident from his indiscriminate pilfering and his sparing of some choice volumes on navigation. In fact his book *Seaman's Secrets* (1595) shows no sign of the material that could have been gleaned from Dee's Library. His practical seamanship fared no better. One expedition to the South Seas (1591-3) was unfortunate. Davis first abandoned his partner and then, after victualling his ship with 14,000 dried penguins, set sail for home and the embrace of a wife who in his absence had taken a lover. His last voyage, to the East Indies, was disastrous, ending with the old sea-dog hacked to death by Japanese pirates in the South China Sea. There is a moral somewhere.

The other culprit got away more or less scot-free. This time the finger points to Nicholas Saunders, or Saunder (1563-1649), a former pupil of John Dee who no doubt knew the value of the Library and helped himself to several hundred books and some of his master's most precious manuscripts and curiosities. A protégé of William Cecil, he even had the nerve to write his name over Dee's, although he was usually more circumspect, bleaching out the name (but still keeping the annotations) and altering the date of ownership. As a recusant Catholic who had changed sides and informed against Jesuits, Saunders had done well for himself as a Member of Parliament for Penrhyn and gaining a knighthood. His Surrey origins – his family was originally from Ewell – were, it is thought by some, the occasion for a feud with the Fromonds of Cheam. It is certainly possible that the Library might have become the battleground. More likely is the idea that Saunders, like Davis, was angered by Dee's sudden withdrawal from navigational projects and simply did not understand the rival attractions of alchemy and angelic discourse in landlocked central Europe. His depredations however do reflect a degree of interest in navigation, although the overall impression is that he simply saw the vulnerable Library as a wide-open opportunity to improve his general reading.

During 1592 however, the year of the *Compendious Rehearsall* and Dee's various attempts at putting his affairs in order, there seems to have been some leverage on Saunders. In his diary for 30 March Dee records:

> *On Thursday Mr Saunders of Ewell sent home my great sea compass but without a needle. It came in the night by water.*

We must make of this what we can. There is however an interesting footnote: today's indirect beneficiaries of Nicholas Saunders' four hundred year old book theft are Christ Church College, Oxford, and the Royal College of Physicians. Is there a moral here as well?

Of course Davis and Saunders might not have been the only culprits, and one certainly cannot dismiss entirely Dee's unsavoury local reputation in certain quarters and the mindless vandalism that an empty house will always attract. A few books were returned by *bona fide* local people such as Mrs Gardner, widow of Robert Gardner; but one cannot avoid the simple fact that Davis and Saunders had appropriated the lion's share. Dee himself was naturally very upset and very suspicious. He insisted on making his own exact inventory with 'this wanteth' against every book or item not yet returned, and was not prepared to let things rest until he had petitioned the Queen to appoint a commission to look into his losses. This was granted on 9 November 1592 and a fortnight later Sir Thomas Gorge and John Walley visited Mortlake. In the *Compendious Rehearsall* Dee claimed that he possessed 4000 books, well in excess of the 2292 volumes of the 1583 catalogue. In fairness Dee also admitted that the missing stock was now down to 500 books, which tends to suggest that many volumes had already been recovered. But the compensation finally awarded by the commission brought Dee only a degree of financial relief, and certainly no offer of any lucrative or stimulating employment.[75] His relations with Nicholas Fromond, even after formal reconciliation and financial settlement, continued frosty. And when Dee finally accepted the post at Manchester, he left no note of the books he was taking or leaving behind. The volumes that did go north, we imagine, would have been only of an everyday usefulness. Even so, Dee was in a position to lend specialist books at the time of the Lancashire witchcraft trial.

After this there is little evidence of any significant library activity, and there is in existence only one book belonging to Dee with an acquisition date between the years 1590 and 1602. The earlier 'spoils' of Davis and Saunders cannot of course account for the loss of later books and so we have to conclude that this solitary volume, given the laws of probability and survival, is a fair reflection of the moribund state of the Library. It all seems to tie in with Dee's increasing poverty and the disappointments that attended his later years. Roberts and Watson certainly consider the possibility that after 1605 books were being sold out of the Library either by Dee himself or, surreptitiously, by his daughter. They also consider Pontoys' custodianship after Dee's death and suggest that during his regular absence in foreign parts there might have been further losses. Pontoys' own death precipitated the major dispersal of the Library in 1625-6, but it is impossible to say precisely which books were stolen during this process and which were acquired legitimately. Roberts and Watson however do provide a working hypothesis as far as the manuscripts are concerned and argue that a single surviving manuscript is much more likely to have been purchased for a purpose than a random loose bundle. The one exception would be Sir Robert Cotton, who legitimately acquired a great many Dee manuscripts in 1621.

The contents of the *Bibliotheca Mortlacensis*, although now widely scattered, survive in surprising numbers to this day. It is perhaps fitting that some of the great libraries of the English-speaking world hold the majority: the British Library, the Bodleian Library, the Cambridge University Library, the Royal College of Physicians and the Wellcome Institute: next the colleges of the two ancient universities: at Cambridge, St John's College (Dee's *alma mater*), Trinity (where he taught Greek), Magdalene and Pembroke: at Oxford, Corpus Christi, Christ Church, Merton and All Souls. Other books are at Yale and in the New York Public Library. One errant volume has even found its way, via Dee's one surviving son, to the University of Basel. The extraordinary thing however is that all these volumes and manuscripts were once part of Elizabethan England's most remarkable library and were located in a small riverside village on the Surrey side of the Thames, not far from London.

---

[70] The facsimile is based on the copy in the Library of Trinity College, Cambridge.

[71] Dee seems to have been Fromond's tenant on his return in late 1589. In March 1592 he paid Fromond a £10 instalment of some kind and yet was 'abominably reviled'.

[72] Bibles, devotional and mystical books, and works of biblical exegesis, as already suggested, might conceivably have been housed in a separate *Bibliotheca interna*.

[73] This was certainly the arrangement in the collection of John Lord Lumley whose 2800 volumes constituted one of the other great Elizabethan libraries.

[74] This is picked up by Dee's first biographer, Thomas Smith. It does the rounds and gains still greater credence by inclusion in Charlotte Fell Smith's important 1909 biography. Finally, the Mortlake mob becomes an entire London crowd in Gwyn Williams' somewhat partisan *Welsh Wizard and British Empire: Dr Dee and a Welsh Identity* (Cardiff, 1980).

[75] Dee had in fact set his heart on the wardenship of St Cross in Winchester, for which he cherished ambitious plans of it becoming a research institute, complete with laboratory and printing press. Its geographical location, he thought, would attract visiting European scholars.

Chapter 5

The Death of Dr John Dee

One tradition has it that Dee saw out his last days, not at the house in Bishopsgate, but at Mortlake with his daughter Katherine. If this is so, it is even possible that he was still barred from the main house by his brother-in-law and was living in the cottage adjoining his laboratories on the other side of the passage leading down to the river.[76] Goodwife Faldo of Mortlake, that amiable and garrulous old crone, interviewed by the Surrey antiquary John Aubrey in 1672, always maintained that her mother had tended Dee during his last illness in his house 'next the house where the tapestry hangings are made'.[77] Dee was certainly without money. The 17th century astrologer William Lily corroborated this and confirmed Mortlake as the place of death:

> *Dr Dee died at Mortlake, Surry, very poor, enforced many times to sell some book or other to buy his dinner with, as Dr Napier of Linford in Buckinghamshire oft related, who knew him very well.*

According to the antiquary Elias Ashmole, it was actually Dee's daughter who was forced to sell the books. When this was discovered, so we are told, the old man was heartbroken.[78]

This same tradition also claims that Dee died in December 1608, the evidence being the Maginus almanac and Dee's crossing off the months until the last illegible entry of 19 December that appears to read *tonitrum a Corrfe* (thunder from?). Thereafter, the almanac seems ominously empty.[79] The Rev WH Yeandle, in *Quadricentennial of the Birth of Dr John Dee*, a brief biography written for the Mortlake Parish Magazine in July 1927, follows this lead and in so doing fixes the year 1608 firmly in Mortlake minds.

But the almanac is not quite so silent, and there is evidence in it to support a later date: 1609. This is the death's head drawn in ink by John Pontoys against 26 March 1609 with the words 'Jno Δ hor. 3 a.m.' (the Greek delta signifying Dee). There is also a separate note from the usually reliable 17th century antiquary Anthony à Wood to Elias Ashmole, confirming that Dee died in London in Bishopsgate.

What is not disputed is that John Dee was buried at the parish church of St Mary the Virgin in Mortlake, though sadly the records do not survive to corroborate this. Tradition has it that his grave was in the chancel and there is no obvious reason to dispute this, although it is just possible that the burial itself was in the churchyard and the brass plate was simply a memorial.[80] John Aubrey certainly thought he had been shown 'Dr Dee's stone' in the chancel by Goodwife Faldo. The brass plate, she said, had disappeared during Oliver Cromwell's time when the minister had levelled the steps at the upper end of the chancel and re-sited the stone.[81] It seems therefore that Aubrey was shown this new location. It is even possible that he was not shown anything remotely plausible: one imagines Goody Faldo embellishing her narrative in every way possible, either to impress her distinguished visitor or to cover the deficiencies of her own failing memory.

This is about as far as we can go regarding the death of Dr John Dee at the age, remarkable for the early 17th century, of eighty-one. Pontoys, who was Dee's heir, was unable to discover any will in the old man's name and John Aubrey came to the same conclusion some fifty years later.[82] But 1608 is unlikely to be the year of Dee's death and Mortlake is almost as unlikely to be the place where it occurred. The thinning-out of the factual record and indeed the whole obscurity and poverty of Dee's last years might point to a deliberate plot against the old man and his estate; but more probable is the simple insight it gives us into the vicissitudes of life, and old age in particular, in Jacobean England. The lack of high-quality historical evidence is at odds with the importance of Dee as an intellectual and scientific phenomenon of Renaissance England.

But Goody Faldo, who as a child had known Dee during these last Mortlake years, did speak of him as 'a mighty good man: a great peacemaker'. Given the extraordinary trajectories of Dee's life, it is perhaps fitting that this charming and authentic recollection has survived in the riverside village where he once lived and of which, for all time probably, he is its most illustrious and unusual resident.

---

[76] The house itself might still have been legally in the hands of Nicholas Fromond, Dee's brother-in-law, who, as we have seen, had advanced money (£400) on the house when Dee left for the Continent.

[77] The Tapestry House, or 'Lower Dutch House', founded in 1619 on the site that is now the green space by the river known as Tapestry Green. It seems perfectly reasonable to suppose that this 'industrial' building was created out of premises that had originally served as Dee's laboratories. John Aubrey (1626-1695), author of *Brief*

Lives, was distantly related to Dee, being the grandson of Dee's cousin, Dr William Aubrey, Vicar of Kew.

[78] Thomas Smith, Dee's first biographer: *Vita Joannes Dee* in *Vitae quorundam eruditissimorum illustrium virorum* (1707).

[79] This is what Charlotte Fell Smith believes in her ground-breaking work, *John Dee* (1909), the first modern biography.

[80] The chancel of Henry VIII's church, not the present chancel which dates from only 1885.

[81] The minister must surely have been the leading non-conformist David Clarkson, ejected in 1662.

[82] No will survives – indeed none could be discovered at Dee's death or in the years following. He died, it seems, very poor. Perhaps there was very little to bequeath. Pontoys in any case appears to have been more Dee's literary executor and custodian of the Library.

Epilogue

In 1642 the confectioner Robert Jones bought a fine cedar chest from a carpenter's shop not far from the Tower of London. He and his wife Susannah then had it moved to their shop in Lombard Street and allowed it to languish during the long years of the Civil War and Commonwealth. In 1662 they decided at last to move the chest. Something rattled inside, and Jones investigated. At the bottom he discovered a small slit, into which he inserted a knife. A secret drawer at once sprang out, revealing about a dozen manuscript books and some olivewood beads attached to a cross, not unlike a rosary.

Jones could make no sense of the papers, but his maid soon found good use for them as pie-linings. She worked her way steadily through half the pile before Jones realised what was happening and returned the surviving papers to the chest.

Jones died in 1664. Two years later the Great Fire gripped the City of London and Susannah Jones was on the point of leaving the heavy chest behind at Lombard Street to burn. Only at the last moment did she remember the papers in the secret drawer and carry them safely to Moorfields, north of the City.

When in due course Susannah remarried she showed the papers to her second husband, Thomas Wale, a warder at the Tower of London who just happened to know a young lawyer who collected old manuscripts.

The name of that young man was Elias Ashmole . . .

Appendix 1

A John Dee Chronology

*This chronology is based loosely on that provided
by Benjamin Woolley in 'The Queen's Conjuror'*

- 13 July 1527: Birth in London
- 1535: Chelmsford Grammar School
- November 1542: St John's College, Cambridge
- 1546: BA
- 1546: Fellow of Trinity College. Under-reader in Greek
- 1548: MA
- 1549: Louvain
- 1550: Lectures in Paris
- 1551-3: Service in aristocratic Protestant circles
- In and out of prison during early reign of Mary
- 1556: Presents plans for national library to Mary
- 1558: Selects auspicious date for Elizabeth's coronation
- January 1559: Coronation of Elizabeth I
- 1563-4: In Europe
- Summer 1564: Presents *Monas Hieroglyphica* to the Queen
- Mid-1560s: Marries Katherine Constable
- 1566: First reference to his living at Mortlake
- 1568: Presented in January to the Queen. Gives her a copy of his work on astronomy/astrology *Propaedeumata Aphoristica* (1558). In February has an audience with her on alchemy
- 1570: Publication of *Mathematicall Praeface* to *Euclid, Elements of Geometrie* (translated by Henry Billingsey)
- 1571: Visits Lorraine to purchase laboratory equipment
- November 1572: A new star, or nova, in Cassiopeia
- 1573: Published book on the nova
- March 1576: Death of wife (first or second?), followed by unexpected visit from the Queen
- February 1578: Second (or third?) marriage, to Jane Fromond
- 1578: Opinion sought on wax effigy discovered of the Queen. Sent also to consult foreign doctors on her illness
- June to October 1579: Mother relinquishes ownership of Mortlake house

- July 1579: Birth of first son, Arthur
- October 1580: Death of mother; again visited by the Queen
- June 1581: Birth of daughter Katherine
- December 1581: Written record of first 'action' with scryer Barnabas Saul
- March 1582: First action with Edward 'Talbot' (Kelley)
- November 1582: Reconciliation with Kelley and receives the sacred show stone'
- January 1583: Birth of son Roland
- February 1583: Consulted by Queen on her proposed marriage to the Duc d'Alençon; submits plans for the reform of the calendar
- March 1583: Visit of emissary from Count Łaski of Poland
- May 1583: Łaski arrives in England, meets Dee at Greenwich
- June 1583: Łaski attends his first 'action'
- September 1583: Leaves for Poland with his family and household. Accompanying him are Kelley and his wife (Joanna), and perhaps Kelley's two step-children
- 1584: Kraków and Prague, audience with the Emperor Rudolf II
- February 1585: Birth of son Michael
- 1585: Back in Kraków. Audience with King Stefan Batory
- 1586: Burning of his books in Prague. Expelled with Kelley from the domains of the Holy Roman Emperor
- September 1586: Under the patronage of Vilém Rožmberk in Bohemia
- April 1587: Kelley proposes 'cross-matching', an exchange of wives
- May 1587: 'Cross matching' pact with Kelley and his wife, Joanna. Last recorded action with Kelley
- February 1588: Birth of son Theodore
- November 1588: Letter to Queen regarding Armada
- February 1589: Kelley leaves Prague
- March 1589: Leaves Bohemia with his family
- December 1589: Reaches Mortlake
- February 1590: Birth of daughter Madimia, named after Madimi, one of the 'angels'
- January 1592: Birth of daughter Frances (Francys)
- 1592: Addresses his *Compendious Rehearsall* to the Queen (an account of his hardships and grievances). In November has an audience with the Queen's commissioners regarding damage at Mortlake during his absence
- May 1594: Audience with the Queen

- June 1594: Visits Archbishop of Canterbury at Croydon with plans to develop the college or almshouses of St Cross at Winchester into a research centre under his wardenship
- July 13 1594: Death of Michael (aged nine)
- August 1595: Birth of final child, Margaret
- October 1595: Dines with Sir Walter Raleigh
- 1595: Supposed death of Kelley
- 1595/6: Possible death of daughter Frances
- February 1596: Takes up the mastership of the collegiate church of Manchester. Difficulties with the fellows. Effectively an exile from London
- 1598-1600: Back in London
- April 1601: Death of son Theodore
- March 1603: Death of Queen Elizabeth
- June 1604: Petitions James I to be cleared of slander
- Spring 1605: Manchester hit by plague. Death of Jane Dee, and possibly the deaths of Roland, Madimia and Margaret, also in Manchester. Only the grown-up children, Arthur and Katherine, survive
- March 1605: Angelic conversations renewed. Failing health
- July 1607: Final 'actions' with Bartholomew Hickman
- 1607?: Buries spirit diaries in the ground at Mortlake
- Dies, probably on 26 March 1609, at the house of John Pontoys in Bishopsgate. Buried in Mortlake, at the parish church of St Mary the Virgin

Appendix 2

The Life of John Dee from John Aubrey's Brief Lives (c.1676)

This Life of Dee is not always easily accessible and for that reason is reproduced here in its entirety. It is characteristically vivid, gossipy, chaotic and inaccurate.

I have left about 1674 with Mr Elias Ashmole three pages in folio concerning him.

The father of this John Dee was a vintner in London (from Elias Ashmole who has it from Dee's grandson). Memorandum: Mr Meredith Lloyd tells me that his father was Roland Dee, a Radnorshire gentleman, and that he has his pedigree, which he has promised to lend me. He was descended from Rees, prince of South Wales. My great grandfather, William Aubrey (LLD), and he were cousins, and intimate acquaintance. Mr Ashmole has letters between them, under their own hands, viz one of Sir William Aubrey to him (ingeniously and learnedly written) touching the *Sovereignty of the Sea*, of which John Dee which he dedicated to Queen Elizabeth and desired my great-grandfather's advice upon it. Dr Aubrey's country house was at Kew, and John Dee lived at Mortlake, not a mile distant. I have heard my grandfather say they were often together.

Arthur Dee, MD, his son, lived and practised at Norwich, an intimate friend of Sir Thomas Browne, MD, who told me that Sir William Boswell, the Dutch ambassador, had all John Dee's manuscripts: ask his executors for his papers. He lived somewhere in Kent.

Ask A. Wood for the manuscripts in the Bodleian Library of Doctor Gwyn, wherein are several letters between him and John Dee, and Doctor Davies, of chemistry and magical secrets, which my worthy friend Mr Meredith Lloyd has seen and read: and he tells me that he has been told that Dr Barlowe gave it to the Prince of Tuscany.

Meredith Lloyd says that John Dee's printed book of spirits is not above the third part of what was written, which were in Sir Robert Cotton's library; many whereof were much perished by being buried, and Sir Robert Cotton bought the field to dig after it.

Memorandum: he told me of John Dee conjuring at a pool in Brecknockshire, and they found a wedge of gold; and that they were troubled and indicted as conjurors at the assizes; that a mighty storm and tempest was raised in harvest time, the country people had not known the like.

His picture in a wooden cut is at the end of Billingsley's *Euclid* but Mr Elias Ashmole has a very good painted copy of him from his son Arthur. He has a very fair, clear sanguine complexion (like Sir Henry Savile); a long beard as white as milk.[83] A very handsome man.

Old goodwife Faldo (a native of Mortlake in Surrey), aged eighty or more (1672), did know Dr Dee, and told me he died at his house in Mortlake, next to the house where the tapestry hangings are made, viz west of that house; and that he died aged about sixty or more, eight or nine years since, and lies buried in the chancel, and had a stone (marble) upon him.[84] Her mother tended him in his sickness. She told me that he did entertain the Polish ambassador at his house in Mortlake, and died not long after; and that he showed the eclipse by means of a *camera obscura* to the said ambassador. She believes that he was eighty years old when he died. She said he kept a great many stills going; that he laid the storm by magic: that the children dreaded him because he was accounted a conjurer. He recovered the basket of clothes stolen when she and his daughter (both girls) were negligent: she knew this . . .

A daughter of his (I think Sarah) is married to a flax-dresser in Southwark: ask for her name.

He built the gallery in the church at Mortlake. Goody Faldo's father was the carpenter that worked on it.

A stone on his grave, which is since removed. At the upper end of the chancel then were steps which in Oliver Cromwell's days were levelled by the minister, and then it was removed. The children when they played in the church would run to Dr Dee's grave stone. She told me that he forewarned Queen Elizabeth of Dr Lopez' attempt against her (the doctor betrayed it, beshit himself).

He used to distil eggshells, and it was from hence that Ben Jonson had his hint of the alchemist, whom he meant.[85]

He was a great peacemaker; if any of the neighbours fell out, he would never let them alone till he had made them friends.

He was tall and slender. He wore a gown like an artist's gown, with hanging sleeves, and a slit.

A mighty good man he was.

He was sent ambassador for Queen Elizabeth (she thinks) into Poland.

Memorandum: his regaining the plate for a certain gentleman's butler, who coming from London by water with a basket of plate, mistook another basket that was like his. Mr J. Dee bid them go by water on such a day, and he would see the man that had his basket, and he did so. But he would not get lost horses, though he was offered several angels (pieces of money). He told a woman (his neighbour) that she laboured under the evil tongue of an ill neighbour (another woman) who came to her house, who, he said, was a witch.

---

[83] This is clearly the portrait of Dee in the Ashmolean Museum, Oxford, reproduced on the front cover.
[84] Dee's death 'aged about sixty or more' is of course completely wrong, and is in fact flatly contradicted a few lines below.
[85] Ben Jonson's comedy of 1610, *The Alchemist*.

Bibliography

Aubrey, John *Brief Lives* (ed. R. Barber, Boydell Press, 1982)

Casaubon, Meric *A True and Faithful Relation of what passed for many years between Dr John Dee and some Spirits* (London, 1659)

Crossley, James (editor) *Autobiographical Tracts of Dr John Dee, Warden of the College of Manchester* (Chetham Society, 1851) [contains *Compendious Rehearsall*]

Clulee, Nicholas H. *John Dee's natural philosophy: Between Science and Religion* (Routledge, London, 1988)

Fell Smith, Charlotte *John Dee* (Constable & Co. London, 1909)

Fenton, Edward (editor) *The Diaries of John Dee* (Day Books, 1998)

Freeman, Leslie *Going to the Parish* (Barnes and Mortlake History Society, 1993)

French, Peter J. *John Dee: the World of an Elizabethan Magus* (Routledge and Keegan Paul, London, 1972)

Grimwade, Mary *Lesser Houses of East Sheen and Mortlake* (Barnes and Mortlake History Society, Occasional Paper Number 10, 2000)

Hailstone, Charles *Alleyways of Mortlake and East Sheen* (Barnes and Mortlake History Society, 1983, reprinted 2009)

Halliwell, James Orchard (editor) *The Private Diary of Dr John Dee* (Camden Society, 1842)

Hancox, Joy *Kingdoms for a Stage, Magicians and Aristocrats in the Elizabethan Theatre* (Sutton Publishing, 2001)

Harkness, Deborah E. *Managing an Experimental Household: The Dees of Mortlake and the Practice of Natural Philosophy* (Isis, Vol.88, no.2, June 1997, pp.247-62)

Harkness, Deborah E. *Shows in the Showstone: A Theater of Alchemy and Apocalypse in the Angel Conversations of John Dee* (*Renaissance Quarterly*, Vol.49, no.4, Winter 1996. pp.707-37)

Harkness, Deborah E. *John Dee's Conversations with Angels* (Cambridge, 1999)

Henrik Jones, Dilys *John Dee, The Magus of Mortlake* (Barnes and Mortlake History Society, Occasional Paper Number 8, 1995)

Meadows, Denis *Elizabethan Quartet* (Longmans, 1956)

Roberts, Julian and Watson, Andrew G. (editors*) John Dee's Library Catalogue* (Bibliographical Society/Oxford University Press, 1990)

Roberts, Julian *Oxford Dictionary of National Biography* (entry on Dee)

Sherman, William H. *John Dee: The Politics of Reading and Writing in the English Renaissance* (University of Massachusetts Press, Amherst, 1995)

Smith, Thomas *Vita Joannes Dee (Vitae quorundam eruditissimorum illustrium virorum,* London, 1707)

Treswell, Ralph *Survey of the Manor of Wimbledon 1617* (original held by the
  Northamptonshire County Record Office, transcript by Raymond Gill in the
  Local Studies Centre, Richmond)
Woolley, Benjamin *The Queen's Conjuror, the Science and Magic of John Dee*
  (Harper Collins, London, 2001)
Yeandle, Rev.W.H. *Quadricentennial of the Birth of Dr John Dee* (Mortlake
  Parish Magazine, offprint, July 1927)

Fiction

Ackroyd, Peter *The House of Dr Dee* (Hamish Hamilton, 1993) [unfortunately
  not set in Mortlake but in the East End of London]
Bowen, Marjorie *I Dwelt in High Places* (Collins, 1933) [from the point of view
  of Jane Dee]

List of Illustrations

Front cover and page 3: Portrait of John Dee by permission of the Ashmolean Museum, Oxford.

Page 6: Mortlake and its environs, drawn by David Deaton

Page 10: John Dee's genealogical notes in *The Laws of Hywel Dada*, by permission of the Wardens and Fellows of Merton College, Oxford.

Page 13: John Dee's diary for November 1577 notes in the margins of Joannes Stadius's *Ephemerides novae* by permission of the Bodleian Library, University of Oxford (Shelf mark: MS Ashmole 487.2v-3r).

Page 14: Title page to Meric Casaubon's *A True and Faithful Relation* (1659) by permission of the Syndics of Cambridge University Library.

Page 17: John Dee's birth chart by permission of the Bodleian Library, University of Oxford (MS Ashmole 1788,fol,137r).

Page 18: Detail from Dee's genealogical roll by permission of the ©British Library Board. (Cotton Charter xiv article 1).

Page 19: St Johns College, Cambridge from David Loggan's *Cantabrigia Illustrata* 1690.

Page 23: *Monas Hieroglyphica* by permission of the ©British Library Board (g718.g.6).

Page 25: The Monad Hieroglyph

Page 26: Richmond Palace etching by Niamh MacGowan, reproduced with the kind permission of the artist (www.niamhmacgowan.com).

Page 29: The frontispiece of Dee's *General and Rare Memorials* (1577), by permission of the ©British Library Board (48.h.18).

Page 31: Edward Kelley a detail from the frontispiece of Meric Casaubon's *A True and Faithful Relation* (1659) by permission of the Syndics of Cambridge University Library.

Page 32: John Dee a detail from the frontispiece of Meric Casaubon's *A True and Faithful Relation* (1659) by permission of the Syndics of Cambridge University Library.

Page 34: Map of Poland

Page 35: Rudolph II

Page 36: Prague in the early seventeenth century

Page 38: Manchester College in the late eighteenth century

Page 40: Dee's petition to James I

Page 44: Map showing the location of Dee's house in Mortlake, adapted by David Deaton from the 1863 Ordnance Survey map

Page 45: A page from Treswell's Survey of the Manor of Wimbledon 1617, by permission of Northamptonshire Record Office, the Spencer Collection.

Page 47: A drawing of Dee's house reproduced in Mary Grimwade's Lesser Houses of East Sheen and Mortlake (BMHS Occasional Papers No.10)

Page 48: Drawing by Milena Dakin depicting a Wealden house suggesting the possible look of Dee's house.

Page 52: Title page of the 1620 edition of of Christopher Marlowe's *Dr Faustus*.

Page 54: Diagram of the Seal of God by permission of the British Library Board (MS Sloane 3188 f.30).

Page 55: Dee's *Holy Table*.

Page 71: Dee's library catalogue by permission of the Master and Fellows of Trinity College, Cambridge.

Photographs on pages 49, 50 and 59 were reproduced by permission of Murray Hedgcock.

Every effort has been made to gain permission to reproduce pictures in this book. If there have been any omissions these will be acknowledged in later editions.

Index

The John Dee of Mortlake Society was founded to mark the 400th anniversary of the death of John Dee in 2009. Details of the Society, its aims and activities can be found on its website:

www.johndeemortlake.org

The Barnes and Mortlake History Society was founded in 1955. It aims to promote interest in the local history of Barnes, East Sheen and Mortlake and to encourage its study. The Society organises lectures on a variety of subjects from local research that touches on individual lives to the broader issues of local history methodology.

Since its inception the Society has produced books and papers on a wide variety of local subjects. These are all available to view at the Local Studies Collection in Richmond. The books are available for loan at Richmond upon Thames libraries or to buy from the Society's website:

www.barnes-history.org.uk